E S S E N T I A L
ROSES

E S S E N T I A L
ROSES
The 100 Best for Design and Cultivation

Text and Photography by Derek Fell

FRIEDMAN/FAIRFAX
P U B L I S H E R S

A FRIEDMAN/FAIRFAX BOOK

© 1990 by Michael Friedman Publishing Group, Inc.

ISBN 1-56799-318-4

Editor: Sharon Kalman
Art Direction: Robert W. Kosturko
Layout: Deborah Kaplan
Photography Director: Christopher C. Bain

Typeset by Mar + x Myles Graphics, Inc.
Color separation by South Sea International Press, Ltd.
Printed and bound in Hong Kong by South China Printing Co. (1988) Ltd.

For bulk purchases and special sales, please contact:
Friedman/Fairfax Publishers
Attention: Sales Department
15 West 26th Street
New York, New York 10010
212/685-6610   FAX 212/685-1307

DEDICATION

For Victoria Rose (Vicki)

ACKNOWLEDGMENTS

Thank you to the many rosarians and owners of rose gardens for allowing me
to photograph their creations, especially to Conard Pyle Company,
West Grove, Pennsylvania; Jackson and Perkins, Medford, Oregon;
and Armstrong Roses, Ontario, California.

9   **INTRODUCTION**

A Salute to the Rose

13   **CHAPTER ONE**

A Rose by any Other Name

ROSE CLASSIFICATIONS
THE STORY OF PEACE ROSE
THE TEN MOST OFTEN ASKED QUESTIONS
   ABOUT ROSES

23   **CHAPTER TWO**

Care of Roses

SOIL PREPARATION
PLANTING ROSES
CONTROLLING INSECTS AND DISEASES
IRRIGATION
WEED CONTROL
PRUNING

33   **CHAPTER THREE**

The Encyclopedia of Essential Roses

99   CHAPTER FOUR

GARDEN PLANS

CUTTING GARDEN FOR ROSES
FRAGRANCE ROSE GARDEN
FLORIBUNDA ROSES
FORMAL PARTERRE GARDEN OF FLORIBUNDA ROSES
OLD-FASHIONED ROSE GARDEN
WAYS TO USE ROSES IN THE LANDSCAPE

113   CHAPTER FIVE

PLANT SELECTION GUIDES

122   APPENDIX ONE

HARDINESS ZONE CHART

124   APPENDIX TWO

SOURCES

126   INDEX OF BOTANICAL AND COMMON NAMES

INTRODUCTION

A SALUTE TO THE ROSE

THE ROSE WAS MADE THE OFFICIAL FLORAL emblem of the United States in 1986 in spite of very strong competition from the marigold, a native North American flowering annual. Rose leaf fossils have been found in Montana and Oregon showing that roses existed on the North American continent 35 to 40 million years ago. The country rejoiced in a well-chosen official flower.

According to mythology, roses were born of the tears shed by the broken-hearted Venus as she wept over her lover, the slain Adonis. Morphologically, the rose is a wonderful example of survival of the fittest, possessing not only thorns for protection against foraging animals, but a cast-iron constitution, beautiful flowers, and wide adaptation. Botanically, garden roses are classified as woody plants—a class that also includes shrubs and trees. Roses belong in the *Rosaceae* family, which includes blackberries, strawberries, cherries, crab apples, firethorn, and hawthorns among its distinguished members.

The rose is believed to be the first flower cultivated by humans. There is evidence that a rose garden was cultivated in Greece in the fifth century BC.

Throughout history, the presence of roses has been recorded at special events. When Christopher Columbus was close to despair at ever finding land during his first voyage to America, his crew picked a rose branch from the water and rejoiced at the possibility that land must be near. It is recorded that when the *Mayflower* landed at Plymouth, Massachusetts, "the shore was fragrant like the smell of a rose garden, and the happy children gathered strawberries and wild roses."

Roses have been cultivated by the Chinese since the Shen Nung Dynasty (2737–2697 BC). However, it was not until the 1700s, when Empress Josephine of France began the first garden—at Malmaison, near Paris—devoted entirely to roses, that roses gained mass appeal in the West. In all, about 250 varieties of roses were planted, and she commissioned a talented artist, Redoute, to paint a magnificent portfolio of the garden. Unfortunately, after the Napoleonic War the garden was neglected, even though interest in roses continued to climb.

It was not until 1910 that efforts were made to restore the rose garden, collecting together as many of the original species and varieties that comprised the original collection as possible.

Modern roses are descended from four wild roses—*Rosa centifolia* (the Cabbage Rose) from Asia, was crossed in 1840 with *R. Chinensis* (the China Rose), producing the first hybrid, called a hybrid perpetual for its ability to bloom more than once. This in turn was crossed with *R. odorata* (the Tea Rose), resulting in a variety called "La France" the first hybrid tea rose.

Roses have the ability to live for a very long time, representing a good investment to the home gardner. A rose bush in Hildeshiem, West Germany, is estimated to be at least 300 years old, while the United States can claim to possess the world's largest rose bush. It is a yellow-flowering Lady Banks Rose in Tombstone, Arizona. Standing 9 feet high with a trunk diameter of 40 inches, it covers an area of 5,380 square feet, supported on a framework of sixty-eight posts. The original cutting came from Scotland in 1884.

This book is intended as a salute to this beautiful plant, with an emphasis on care, planting ideas, and recommended selections for what can be described as "the world's most beautiful flower".

Left: By grafting it onto a long stem, this beautiful shrub rose has been trained to form a tree shape. It is one of many planted in the garden of French painter Claude Monet, at Giverny. *Right top:* The old-fashioned Moss Rose has a strong fragrance. *Right bottom:* The miniature rose, 'Magic Carousel' is a beautiful pink-and-white bicolor that makes a lovely houseplant if placed in a sunny location. *Far right:* The elegant arching cane of the white Cherokee rose is studded with large single flowers that contrast beautifully with the dark water of a stream.

CHAPTER ONE

A ROSE BY ANY OTHER NAME

Roses are sold through retail stores, such as garden centers, and by mail order from catalogs. They are available either "bare-root" or "potted". If you buy a bare-root rose, the canes are cut short and may have a wax coating that acts as an anti-desiccant to resist dehydration. The roots are washed clean of soil, packed in moist sphagnum moss, and enclosed in a plastic wrapper.

There are three grades of bare-root roses, but in general the home gardener should choose #1 grade. The other grades (#1 $\frac{1}{2}$ and #2) are inferior and not worth risking the time and effort needed for planting and care.

Potted plants are grown in a disposable container rooted in a potting soil. Though potted plants may appear to offer a higher survival rate, the better buy is usually a dormant bare-root plant, planted during the bare-root season, which generally runs October through April in cold climates and December through February in areas where freezing does not occur. Outside the bare-root season, roses can be bought potted for transplanting into the garden in the spring.

To help make selections, even if you intend buying from a local retail store, obtain some rose catalogs and study the descriptions. They generally list the name, type, growth habit, color, and price. Some may indicate specific climatic

requirements, but for specific information on the best roses for your particular area, visit local rose gardens, attend a meeting of the local Rose Society, or consult a friend with growing experience.

A list of mail order sources is given in the source section, page 124.

Two excellent sources of worthwhile, old-fashioned roses are Tillotson's (also called Roses of Yesterday and Today) and the Antique Rose Emporium; see listings in the source section, page 124.

Height Standards For the purpose of describing relative heights among roses, the American Rose Society has designated three groups:

Low: Under 30 inches ($1\frac{1}{2}$ feet)
Medium: 30 to 48 inches ($1\frac{1}{2}$ to 4 feet)
Tall: Over 48 inches (4 feet)

It must be realized that these broad designations are based on national averages, and under optimum conditions a rose described as medium height may in fact exceed 4 feet, while a rose described as low-growing may exceed $1\frac{1}{2}$ feet.

National Ratings The American Rose Society conducts a rating system from 1 to 10 for all roses available to buy and publishes the list annually. Because of climatic differences in North America, some chapters of the American Rose Society (such as the San Francisco Rose Society) have established rating systems independent of the National system, and wherever possible gardeners should seek local ratings. However, the National ratings system does help to show those plants that are generally widely adaptable. The roses are judged by the following categories: novelty, bud form, flower form, color opening, color finishing, substance, fragrance, habit, vigor, foliage, disease resistance, flowering effect, and overall value. The ratings are scored as follows:

10.0 Perfect (to date, no rose is rated 10)
9.9-9.0 Outstanding
8.9-8.0 Excellent
7.9-7.0 Good
6.9-6.0 Fair
5.9 or less   Poor, of questionable value

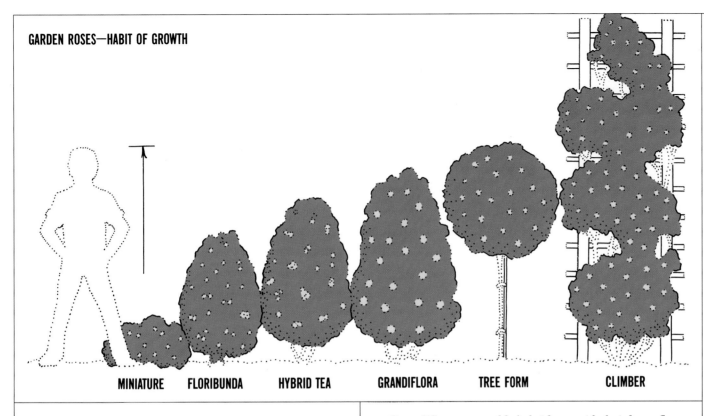

GARDEN ROSES—HABIT OF GROWTH

MINIATURE   FLORIBUNDA   HYBRID TEA   GRANDIFLORA   TREE FORM   CLIMBER

Opposite page: The climbing rose, Constance Spry, decorates the side of a barn. Flower arrangers love this rose for its heavenly fragrance and double, cupped, old-fashioned flowers. *Left*: This drawing illustrates the approximate growing sizes of the six different types of roses. Climbing roses will continue to grow upward as long as they have something to anchor onto.

ROSE CLASSIFICATIONS

The American Rose Society has established standards for classifying roses. In addition to categorizing roses by plant habit (grandifloras, floribundas, climbers, etc.), the Society has standardized color classifications, height comparisons, and has devised a rating system from 1 to 10 of overall performance as a result of tests conducted by rose growers throughout the country.

The following classifications describe roses by type:

Hybrid Teas are large-flowered roses growing one bloom to a stem. The term "tea" comes from their derivation from the "tea rose of China," which possesses a distinctive tealike fragrance. They are called hybrids because they are all the product of man-made crosses (hybridizing) between selected parents. Hybrid teas are mostly used as specimens for garden display and for cutting.

Grandifloras resemble hybrid teas with their large flower size, but their flowers differ in that they are held above the plant in clusters, rather than atop long, single stems. Grandifloras tend to grow tall and are best used as backgrounds.

Polyanthas are a strain of old-fashioned roses that date back hundreds of years. They bear small flowers that are produced in dense clusters. Many are highly subject to mildew, but are important parents in the development of the next classification, floribundas. Polyanthas are mostly used for hedges and singly to produce a shrub effect.

Floribundas have larger flowers than polyanthas, but not as large as grandifloras or hybrid teas, and they produce their flowers in clusters. Floribundas are excellent for massing in beds and borders.

Climbers are mostly mutations of polyanthas, grandifloras, hybrid teas, and floribundas, producing abnormally long canes that can be trained to climb. They can be trained vertically and horizontally.

Right: This drawing illustrates the anatomy of the rose. Basically, all roses have the same anatomy. *Opposite page:* This drawing represents the eight types of rose blossoms typical to most garden roses.

ANATOMY OF A ROSE

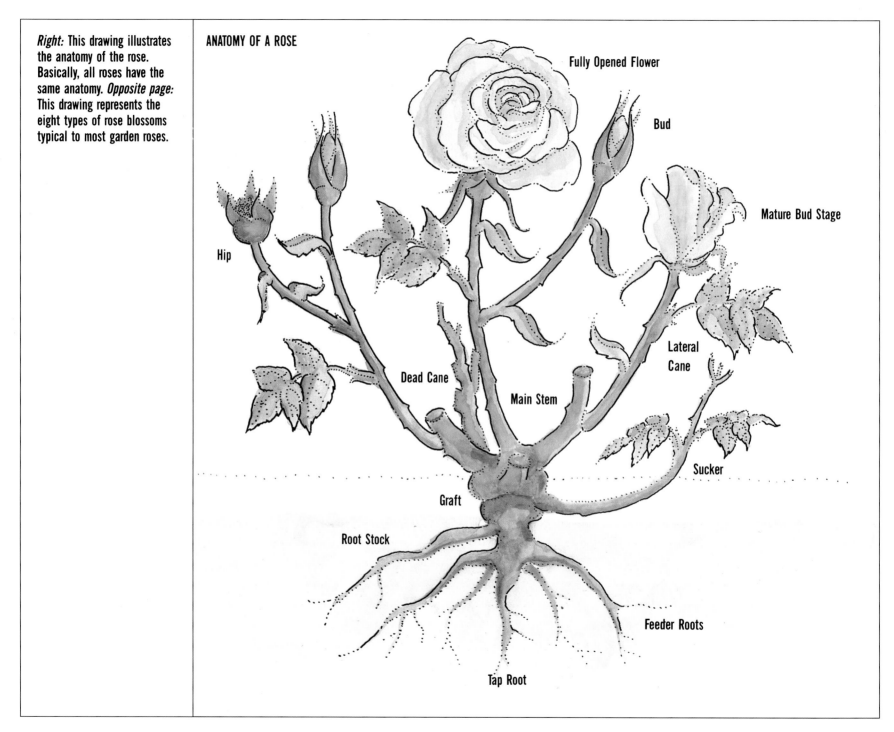

Fully Opened Flower

Bud

Mature Bud Stage

Hip

Lateral Cane

Dead Cane

Main Stem

Sucker

Graft

Root Stock

Feeder Roots

Tap Root

Hybrid Tea

Single-flowered

Climber
(cluster-flowered)

Floribunda
(clusters)

Miniature

Semi-double

Grandiflora

Minatures are tiny roses that grow on dwarf, compact plants, developed from a sophisticated breeding program involving old polyanthas, floribundas, and wild roses with especially small flower forms. They are excellent for growing in containers, creating a low ground cover effect, and decorating sunny rooms as houseplants.

Miscellaneous Shrub Roses is a "catch-all" category for roses that generally do not seem to fit into the other main groups. Some of these include Pillar roses (short climbers) and some hedge roses that are too tall to be called miniatures and too small to be called polyanthas or floribundas.

In addition to these six basic rose classifications, we hear a lot about other designations. For example, there are species roses, which are roses found in the wild. Some of the most popular for garden culture are *Rosa centifolia* (Cherokee Rose), *Rosa rugosa* (Rugosa Rose) and *Rosa banksea* (Lady Banks Rose).

Old-fashioned Roses lump together a whole host of old cultivated roses with an obscure parentage. These include Moss Roses, with a mosslike covering on the flower buds, Damask Roses, named for their heady fragrance, and Gallicas, famous in Tudor times as the Rose of York (a pink) and the Rose of Lancaster (a white), the floral symbols used by opposing armies in Britain's Civil War, known as the War of the Roses. Few old-fashioned roses are grown in home gardens because of their relatively sparse flowers and rangy habit, but they still make their ways into historic gardens and special rose collections. There are a few exceptions to this generalization, including Roi de Victoria (a pink) and Cardinal de Richelieu (a purple). They are reasonably free-flowering with cup-shaped, fragrant, multi-layered flowers liked especially by flower arrangers. The individual rose descriptions in Chapter Three list the ratings from the National Rose Society.

All-American Rose Selections is a non-profit organization consisting of judges with rose test gardens. These gardens are located in different climatic regions of North America. Each year the judges grow and evaluate new roses sent from breeders in different countries. They grow the entries alongside roses already in commerce and give them points in comparison to these. The points are totalled and those with the required number of points receive either a bronze, silver, or gold medal and are introduced to the general public with a fanfare of publicity. All-America Selections does not test miniatures, but the American Rose Society makes "Awards of Excellence" in this category. A list of All-America Award winners appears on pages 120–121.

THE STORY OF PEACE ROSE:
French Breeding Expertise and American Salesmanship Combine to Create the Rose Sensation of All Time

The story of Peace Rose, the most famous rose in the history of modern rose breeding, began in 1935 when Papa Meilland, head of the French rose breeding concern of Meilland & Son, helped his son, Francis, select fifty promising seedlings for evaluation from a cross-pollination program. These fifty were culled from a total of eight hundred that had been patiently grown from seed to flower. They assigned each seedling a number so that they could refer to their notebooks and tell what particular cross produced any one of the fifty seedlings.

As was customary, at the start of every blooming season the Meillands invited a group of rose experts from around the world to inspect their test plots. From these visits the Meillands could often tell if a particular rose caught their fancy and helped the family decide which to introduce into cultivation.

The date was June 1939—three months before the outbreak of World War II. The star of the show was a plant innocuously labelled 3-35-40. The blooms of 3-35-40 were an incredible size—bigger than anything previously seen in a hybrid tea. The stems were strong, the leaves exuded health and vigor, a shimmering dark green, but most important of all was its enchanting color, marked by its romantic aura. The light yellow petals were shaded from pale ivory at the center to clear golden yellow at the edges, the tips were suffused with a touch of pink deepening to carmine. Every flower that opened, from bud to petal drop, was pure perfection, fully double, high pointed in the bud stage; it unfolded slowly, and outlasted every other rose in cultivation. To crown it all, the plants were extraordinarily hardy.

In spite of the dark political situation that was threatening the world with war, the success of 3-35-40 among the visiting rose experts suffused the Meilland family with a sense of happiness and tranquility. They knew that they had an extraordinary world-class rose on their hands. All it needed now was to be islolated and propagated into dozens, then hundreds, and finally thousands of cuttings so enough plants could be sold to start giving the family a return on their investment.

Unfortunately, war was not a good time to be selling roses, and by the day rose shipments were embargoed (a result of the outbreak of World War II) only three shipments of 3-35-40 had been sent out: one to a rose grower in Germany, another to a grower in Italy, and a third to Mr. Robert Pyle, head of the Conard Pyle Company, a rose grower located near Philadelphia, Pennsylvania. In the rush to send out these precious shipments, rose 3-35-40 had no name, even

though the Meilland family had decided, in one of their brainstorming sessions, to call the new rose Madame A. Meilland after Papa Meilland's mother.

As news came back about the shipments, the Meillands learned that the German grower had bestowed on the new rose the name, Gloria Dei (Glory be to God) while the Italian grower had called it Gioia!, meaning Joy; no immediate news was received of the American shipment. To survive the war, they devoted most of their rose fields to raising vegetables.

Finally, a month to the day after the liberation of France, a letter arrived at the Meilland household from America. It was from Robert Pyle, and his words were like music. He wrote: "My eyes are fixed in fascinated admiration on a glorious rose, its pale gold, cream and ivory petals blending to a lightly ruffled edge of delicate carmine . . . I am convinced it will be the greatest rose of the century."

Pyle had arranged a "Name Giving Ceremony" for the new rose at the Pacific Rose Society's Exhibition at Pasadena, California on Sunday, April 29, 1945. The war still raged in Europe, and after consulting with other rose growers, Pyle drafted a statement that was to be read at the Exhibition. It said: "We are decided that this greatest new rose of our time should be named for the world's greatest desire: PEACE."

Sunday, April 29, 1945 dawned bright and clear in Pasadena for the conference of rose growers. As the name for the new rose was declared, two white doves were set free. Miraculously, in war-weary Europe, after six long years, a truce was declared. The bombs stopped. On the day the Peace Rose was named, World War II ended and the world was at peace.

More coincidences followed. On the day that the judges for All-America Rose Selections met and honored Peace with an award, the war in Japan ended. A month later, on the day a peace treaty was signed in Japan, the American Rose Society bestowed its highest award on the Peace Rose: a gold medal.

Within a period of nine years, thirty million Peace Roses were planted throughout the world, each of them the progeny of a single seed no bigger than a pinhead, that produced a seedling known simply as 3-35-40 until it flowered 5,000 miles away on a Pennsylvania farm, inspiring a conservative Quaker businessman, Robert Pyle, to grant it a name nobody could ever forget, the Peace Rose.

THE TEN MOST OFTEN ASKED QUESTIONS ABOUT ROSES

1. **WHAT IS THE MOST POPULAR ROSE VARIETY OF ALL?**
The yellow-and-pink hybrid tea rose called Peace, developed by the firm of Meilland in France. However, in recent years, there has been extraordinary interest in climbing roses and in hedge roses. The climber, Blaze, has started to exceed sales of Peace, as has the hedge rose Simplicity.

2. **HOW SOON AFTER PLANTING WILL ROSES BE IN BLOOM?**
Floribunda, hybrid tea, and hedge roses will bloom just six to eight weeks after planting. Climbers will bloom a little during the first season, but are at their best by the second year. For more on planting roses, see pages 23–24.

3. **CAN I GROW ROSES IN CONTAINERS?**
Yes, roses can be grown in containers. Miniature roses and small floribundas are easiest, but even hybrid teas will do nicely in planter boxes. See page 111 for specific container planting ideas.

4. **WHY ARE MY ROSES MORE FRAGRANT AT CERTAIN TIMES?**
Roses are often more fragrant on warm, humid days and during a brief time before a summer storm. Drought, extreme heat, or very cool days diminish their fragrance.

5. **WHAT ARE THE MOST FRAGRANT ROSES?**
Fragrant Cloud, Fragrant Memory, Intrigue, Dolly Parton, and Tropicana are among the most fragrant varieties. For a larger listing see page 119.

6. **HOW DO I KNOW IF ROSES WILL GROW IN MY AREA?**
Roses are extremely hardy plants and will grow in just about any area of North America. In the most northern areas, however, plants may require some winter protection, such as mulching around the roots after the ground freezes.

7. **WHEN IS THE BEST TIME OF YEAR TO TRANSPLANT ROSES?**
The best time to transplant is either in the fall or in the early spring when roses are dormant and the ground is workable.

8. **WHEN IS THE BEST TIME TO PRUNE ROSES?**
The best time for pruning is early spring, sometime after the last killing frost, and just before new growth starts. For more about pruning see page 29.

9. **WHERE CAN I PLANT ROSES?**
Roses can be planted in any location that meets the following three requirements: The spot must receive at least four to six hours of direct sun each day; there must be enough space to allow 18 to 24 inches around the plant for air circulation; and the soil must drain well enough that there is no standing water. For complete planting instructions see pages 23–24.

10. **HOW MUCH TROUBLE IS IT TO GROW ROSES?**
Though protected from foraging animals by thorns, the succulent leaves are subject to attack by insects and diseases and a spray program is advisable. A regular feeding program and irrigation also help produce superlative results. For complete care instructions see pages 24–29.

Opposite page: A beautiful close-up of Peace rose, which captivated the hearts of the world after World War II.

Left: The climbing rose, America, scrambles along a fence, displaying its large, fragrant double blooms. Right: A bed of hybrid tea roses line a driveway leading to a private home.

CHAPTER TWO

CARE OF ROSES

Good soil is essential for quality rose plants. If the soil is not properly prepared no amount of fertilizing, irrigation, or spraying will yield superior results. Soil not only serves to anchor a rose plant, it provides nutrients to roots. Nutrients enter the roots in *soluble* form; therefore, the soil must have good moisture-holding capacity, yet allow excess water to drain.

SOIL PREPARATION

Soil that puddles because of poor drainage can be improved by laying a bed of crushed stones on top of it and building a raised soil bed with landscape ties above the water table. Another alternative is to drain the area.

Sand, clay, and loam are the three main types of soil. Sand has poor anchorage and lets moisture and nutrients drain away too rapidly; it trickles through the fingers when held in the hand. Clay is thick, sticky, and cold, forming tight wads when squeezed in the hand. Roots find it hard to penetrate the suffocating, airless mass represented by clay. Loam is a happy medium, not too light and not too heavy, containing generous amounts of organic matter to make it fluffy.

To improve a soil that is too sandy or one that is composed of too much clay, the remedy is the same—generous amounts of compost must be added to boost its organic content. Fail-

ing a supply of compost, add well-rotted manure, well-decomposed leaf mold, or bales of peat instead.

Poor soils are best improved in autumn, prior to spring planting, allowing the soil conditioners time to interact with the original soil base and to build up populations of beneficial soil bacteria.

The best test for good soil is the squeeze test. Take a handful of moist soil and squeeze it tight. When you open your hand, the soil should not bind together like clay, nor run through your fingers like sand. It should just remain as loose and crumbly after squeezing as before.

It doesn't pay to be complacent about good soil. The action of wind, rain, and footprints on soil will lead to compaction and the natural feeding of roots will deplete nutrients. Adding a commercial fertilizer each year is not enough; the addition of humus each autumn is also a necessity.

PLANTING ROSES

The best size for a planting hole (except for miniature roses) is 2 feet wide by 1¹/₂ feet deep. This represents the removal of approximately forty gallons of soil. A good soil mix for the planting hole is comprised of 20 percent humus in the form of compost, leaf mold or peat; 20 percent well-decomposed horse or cow manure; and 60 percent garden topsoil. In the

PLANTING A ROSE (Right):

1—This is a typical bare-root plant ready for planting.

2—Dig a hole to accommodate the spread and depth of roots. Mound soil in the bottom of the hole and spread the roots over the mound.

3—Leave a 1-inch lip around hole to catch water.

4—Mound wood-chip mulch around the base of the plant.

absence of animal manure, double up on the humus and add a 5-10-5 granular fertilizer to the mix.

With the soil mix described above, build a cone in the bottom of the hole so that the roots of a bare-root plant can be spread evenly and the bud union (an enlarged section between the root section and branches) sits slightly above the level of the soil surface. Keeping the plant upright, shovel soil over the roots and tamp the soil down with your feet to settle it and make contact around the roots (see diagrams, page 25).

With a potted rose plant there is no need to build a cone. Simply shovel soil into the bottom of the hole until you can place the top of the root ball level with the soil surface. Fill around the sides, tamping the loose soil so the root ball sits tightly in the hole.

Give each plant four gallons of water. When all settling has stopped it may be necessary to adjust the bud union so it sits above the soil line.

In northern states, where winters are severe and roses are planted in the autumn, it is essential to build a mound of soil to 8 or 9 inches above the bud union for protection against "winterkill"—the drying effects of cold winter winds and glaring sun.

Fertilizing

Before the soil is mounded, a slow-release, high-phosphorus fertilizer (such as 5-10-5) can be added to the soil surface. After the plant has leafed out and finished blooming, a regular feeding schedule can be practiced.

A basic fertilizing program should consist of the following: Surface feeding with a 5-10-5 or 10-20-10 slow release fertilizer at time of planting (spring or fall), and a booster application in spring and autumn each year thereafter. Different brands of fertilizer require different amounts of application, so read the label carefully. In addition to granular fertilizer, it's possible to keep roses fed by foliar feeding by spraying a liquid fertilizer onto leaf surfaces.

The best rose fertilizers have a 1-2-1 ratio of plant nutrients, such as 10-20-10 or 15-30-15. These numbers stand for the percentages of vital plant nutrients, nitrogen, phosphorus, and potassium, in that order. Nitrogen grows lush leaves, phosphorus develops a healthy root system and encourages flower bud formation, and potassium adds overall vigor. The rest is "filler" used as a distributing agent.

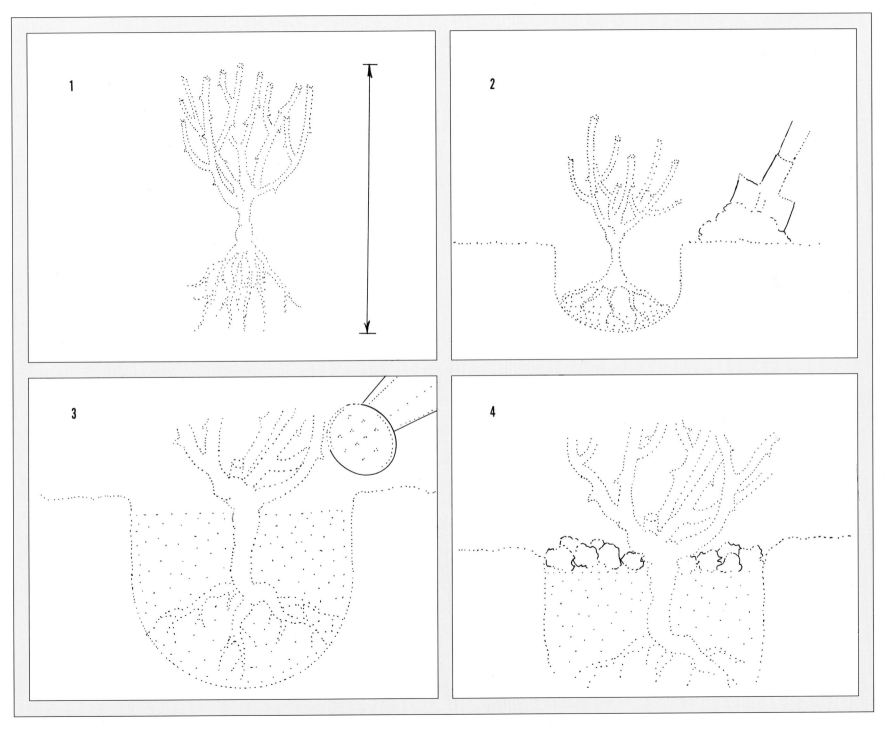

CONTROLLING INSECTS AND DISEASES

Though roses have developed a good defense—their thorns—against foraging animals, the leaves are especially susceptible to attack by insects and diseases. The old saying, "an ounce of prevention is worth a pound of cure," is particularly true with roses, since once a problem occurs it is often difficult to eradicate.

Good soil, topped up annually to maintain its humus content, a regular feeding schedule, and irrigation during dry spells will help give roses a strong constitution to resist diseases, but a precautionary spray program involving the following is also advisable:

Insecticide Harmful insect pests either chew leaves or suck their juices. The biggest enemies of roses are aphids, scale, and Japanese beetles.

Miticide Spider mites are tiny creatures that build fine webbing among foliage and suck a plant's juices. Ordinary insecticides are usually ineffective in controlling them, so a miticide is needed.

Fungicide Roses are attacked mainly by three fungi: mildew, blackspot, and rust. Mildew is a silvery, dusty coating on leaf surfaces that inhibits the manufacture of chlorophyll, thus weakening plants. Blackspot consists of small, black marks covering leaf surfaces and a yellowing of the leaf. Rust is evident by brownish pustules covering leaf surfaces.

Though there are different sprays available for each problem listed above, it is possible to buy chemical controls that are pre-mixed so a general purpose insecticide, miticide, and fungicide can be applied at one time.

It's also possible to use specific organic controls. For example, some roses are resistant to blackspot and mildew. Insecticidal soaps and also pyrethrum/rotenone sprays or dusts are available. These products are not long-lasting in their control, but they are environmentally safe, leaving no harmful residues to contaminate the soil.

Irrespective of what kind of spray product you choose, always read the label carefully before use, since dosages differ and even sprays made from "organic" compounds may be toxic to humans, pets, or fish.

IRRIGATION

Roses require watering during dry spells, and by far the most efficient way to water roses is by means of a drip irrigation system. Many kinds of drip lines are available, costing as little as $25.00 to irrigate 500 square feet, to over $100.00. There are two basic kinds. The "emitter" type has small nozzles spaced at two feet intervals to drip water from each nozzle. Another type has micro-pores along the hose length so it "sweats" beads of moisture from beginning to end.

Most drip irrigation lines can be laid on the soil surface and simply covered with a light layer of mulch to hide them.

Drip lines are connected to a water source, allowing you to turn on a faucet, leave it on overnight, and turn it off in the morning. Some can be fitted with a fertilizer applicator so that the water mixes with plant nutrients to feed plants while they are being watered.

WEED CONTROL

Rose beds should be kept free of weeds. The easiest way to do this is by laying down a mulch around the plants. A mulch is a covering that rests on top of the soil. It can be organic, such as wood chips, pink bark, or shredded leaves, or it can

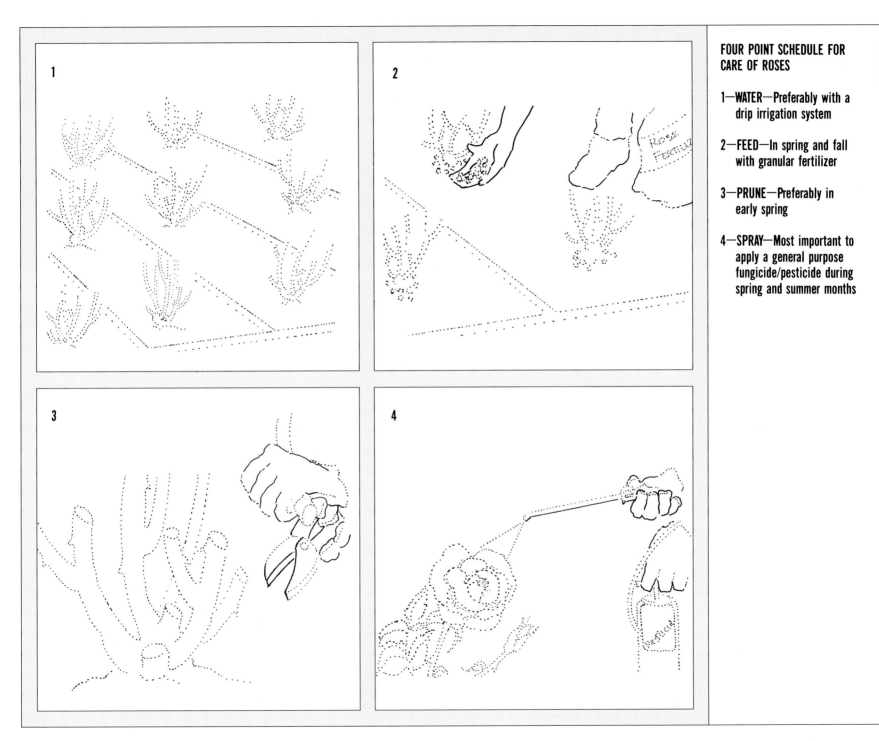

FOUR POINT SCHEDULE FOR CARE OF ROSES

1—WATER—Preferably with a drip irrigation system

2—FEED—In spring and fall with granular fertilizer

3—PRUNE—Preferably in early spring

4—SPRAY—Most important to apply a general purpose fungicide/pesticide during spring and summer months

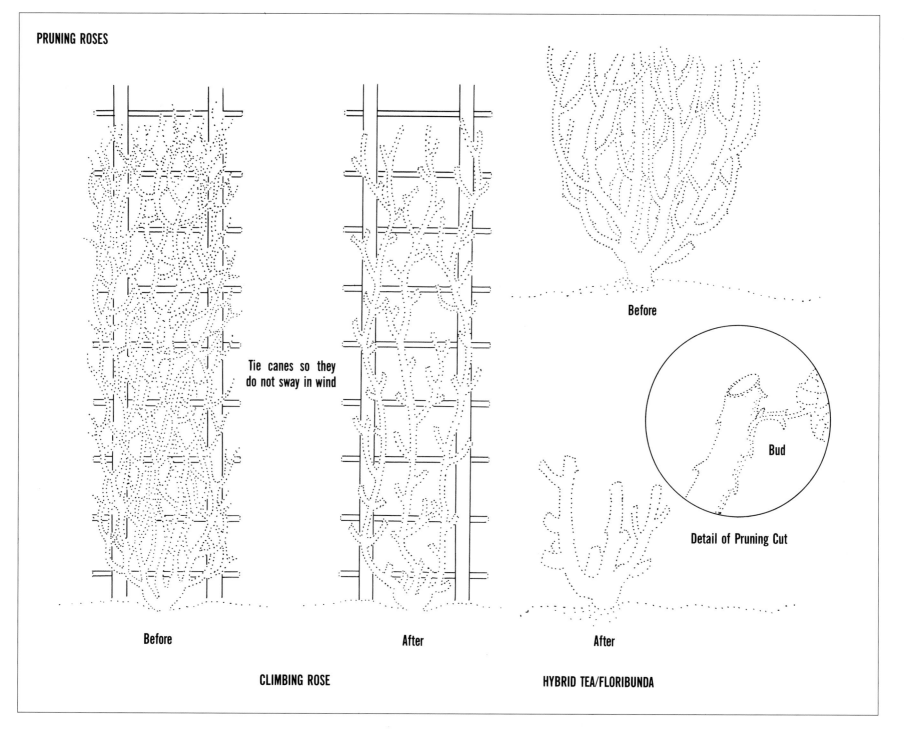

Tie canes so they
do not sway in wind

Before

Before

Bud

After

After

Detail of Pruning Cut

CLIMBING ROSE

HYBRID TEA/FLORIBUNDA

be non-organic, such as black plastic. Mulching not only acts as a weed barrier, it reduces moisture evaporation and stabilizes soil temperatures, cooling soil in the case of organic mulches like wood chips, heating it up in the case of black plastic. Since roses prefer a cool soil temperature, organic mulches are preferred. If black plastic is used, it should be covered with an organic mulch to break the sun's rays.

Organic mulches may need "topping up" during the growing season, since decomposition depletes the supply, which is itself a benefit since it adds valuable humus to the soil as it decomposes.

PRUNING

It is necessary to prune roses for several reasons: to stimulate the production of new canes, since the best roses tend to be produced on new canes (all desirable new canes are produced *above* the bud union); to eliminate suckers (suckers originate from *below* the bud union), since suckers rob the plant of energy; to control the plant's height or shape; and to remove dead or crowded canes.

Proper pruning keeps the center of the plant open to encourage light penetration and air movement.

It is essential after pruning to remove all canes and fallen leaves to a compost pile, or burn them since this debris can harbor diseases if left around the plants.

Examine the accompanying diagrams showing how to prune a rose for the desired effect.

The best time for pruning depends on where you live. In areas with winter freezes, pruning should begin when the spring thaw begins and before the leaf buds have started to open out. Pruning too early can weaken the plant. In areas with mild winters pruning is generally done in January or February.

The most important tool for pruning roses is a hand pruner, particularly one with a curved "anvil" blade that makes a clean cut and resists tearing tissue. These are good for pruning canes up to $1/2$-inch thickness. Next is a long-handled lopper, good for pruning canes thicker than $1/2$ inch, and also for reaching into dense growth to open up a "window" so a hand pruner can be used.

Many rose growers also like to use a pruning saw especially the kind with a scimitar or crescent-shaped blade that folds into the handle, allowing for precision cuts when removing suckers or canes that are close to the bud union. A heavy pair of gauntlet-type gloves is a necessity for pruning in order to avoid being scratched by large thorns.

When making cuts to canes it is best to make them on a slant, pointing down from the opposite side of a leaf bud in order to shed water away from the bud. A discerning eye is needed before making any drastic cuts. First take out all dead canes, then remove all undersized canes or "whips," canes less than the thickness of a pencil. Next, decide what lateral canes to keep for good shape and which to remove for good air circulation. Try not to cut into the main canes. These are the prime source of energy and new canes, and too heavy a pruning hand on these may drastically weaken the plant. When cutting healthy canes, make the cut no more than 1 inch above a leaf bud. If the cut is made too high, dieback may occur in the exposed stump, and pose a danger of it continuing to the full length of the cane. If cut too close to the leaf bud, a new lateral cane may fail to develop.

When lateral canes emerge from below the main canes, it is generally best to regard these as new main canes and preserve them. At least do not prune them back lower than the level of the original main canes.

Pruning Climbers

The foregoing pruning tips refer especially to hybrid tea roses, polyanthas, grandifloras, and floribundas. With climbing roses, the object is to preserve the length of the best canes and encourage maximum bloom production on these selected canes. Generally speaking, climbers should be pruned of all upright growth except four to six strong, healthy canes after they have gone dormant in autumn. The remaining canes should be secured fast to their support, and in areas with harsh winters, the lower regions should be wrapped in burlap sacking to resist dehydration from cold winds or glaring sun and subsequent dieback.

Left: In late April and early May, the city gardens in Charleston, South Carolina, overflow with roses; here, they are planted in gardens and over a trellis.

HOW TO HYBRIDIZE A ROSE

Roses are one of the easiest of plants to hybridize. You don't need to be a professional rose grower to create a new rose. Here, in words and pictures, is how to do it yourself.

1. First, select your parents. This is the female parent. Take a mature bud and open up the petals to reveal the center circle of pollen-bearing anthers. Using tweezers, remove the ring of anthers (the male part of the flower) so pollen from them does not pollinate the central cluster of stigmas (the female part of the flower). This part is called "the emasculation".

2. Collect pollen from another flower (the male parent) by placing the pollen-laden anthers in a jar and storing them in a refrigerator until ready to use.

3. Using a camel's hair brush, transfer pollen from the jar to the stigmas of the female parent. This part is called "the cross".

4. Tag the crosses with the names of the parents and dates of the cross. For example, if you crossed 'Iceberg' floribunda rose (the female parent) with 'Showbiz' floribunda rose (the male parent), make a tag saying 'Iceberg (female) x Showbiz' (male).

5. As the seed pods (the hips) ripen, collect the seeds and plant into potting soil. As the seeds germinate, grow them to transplant size and transfer to the garden for evaluation.

6. As the seedlings bloom, check them to see if any are worth saving and propagating. If they are, give each hybrid a name and increase the number of plants by taking cuttings.

CHAPTER THREE

THE ENCYCLOPEDIA OF ESSENTIAL ROSES

PRESENTED IN THIS CHAPTER ARE 100 CHOICE roses, ranging from the large-flowering hybrid teas to the dainty, diminutive miniatures, including old-fashioned roses, wild species roses, and roses for special landscape effects, such as hedging roses.

Heights given are approximate and will vary according to climate and the fertility of the soil. Generally, fertile soils, especially those fertilized with animal manure, can produce much taller plants than specified here.

It is impossible in a book of this scope to include every garden-worthy variety, especially of a class like floribunda roses and hybrid teas, each of which includes more than a thousand varieties still in general commerce. Selections have been made primarily to offer a range of colors, and to provide those which have the greatest popular appeal.

The photographs are mostly close-ups in actual garden settings, in natural light on a slightly overcast day. Bright sunlight and indoor lighting can change the appearance of rose colors dramatically.

The roses in this section are divided alphabetically by major class, as follows:

Hybrid Tea Roses . . . . .Page 34
Floribunda Roses . . . . .Page 52
Grandiflora Roses . . . . .Page 62
Climbing Roses . . . . .Page 68
Miniature Roses . . . . .Page 76
Hedge Roses . . . . .Page 82
Old-Fashioned Roses . . . . .Page 84
Species Roses . . . . .Page 90

HYBRID TEA ROSES

The largest-flowering of all roses, growing one big bloom on a single stem, generally held erect. The term "Tea" comes from the distinctive tealike fragrance of the flowers. They are all careful, man-made crosses, usually involving other hybrid tea varieties or else seedlings produced from these varieties. In the garden, hybrid teas are generally used for massing together in a bed or border. The flowers are valued by flower arrangers who like to pick the flowers in what is called the "mature bud" stage—halfway between a tight bud formation and an open flower.

Below is the hybrid tea rose, Heirloom.

NAME Blue Moon

RATING ARS 7.4; Gold Medal Rome, 1964.

TYPE Hybrid Tea

ORIGIN Introduced in 1964. Produced in Germany by the House of Tantau from crossing Sterling Silver and an unnamed seedling.

HEIGHT 5 feet; upright, vigorous habit. Climbing Blue Moon, a mutation of Blue Moon, grows much taller.

FRAGRANCE Pleasant, heavy fragrance.

DESCRIPTION Considered one of the very best blue roses, which are not a true blue, but more of a lavender-blue. The large, 4-inch double blooms are produced singly on strong stems. Foliage is dark green, leathery, and disease-resistant. Makes an attractive cut flower in the mature-bud stage. Seems to prefer warmer climates.

NAME Brandy

RATING ARS 7.3; AARS Award, 1982.

TYPE Hybrid Tea

ORIGIN Introduced by Armstrong Nurseries in 1982. A cross between First Prize and Dr. A. J. Verhage.

HEIGHT 4 to 5 feet; upright, bushy habit.

FRAGRANCE Mild, tealike fragrance.

DESCRIPTION Large, bronze, double, golden-apricot blooms develop from long, streamlined buds. Vigorous plants with semi-glossy, dark green leaves. Disease-resistant. Highly valued by flower arrangers for the perfection of its flowers, especially in the mature-bud stage. Often sold as "sweetheart" roses.

NAME Candy Stripe

RATING ARS 6.5.

TYPE Hybrid Tea

ORIGIN Introduced in 1963 by Conard Pyle Co. A mutation of pink Peace.

HEIGHT Up to 4 feet; bushy habit.

FRAGRANCE Pleasant, heavy fragrance.

DESCRIPTION Large, double blooms of dusky pink streaked almost white, measures up to 6 inches across. Profuse blooming. Glossy, dark green, leathery leaves. No rose breeder has yet developed a really good red-and-white bicolored rose, with uniform candy-cane striping. The public would love it, especially as a climber. Candy Stripe and a similar rose named Candystick (also known as Red 'n White Glory) come the closest in uniformity. Candystick was hybridized by J. B. Williams and released through Lakeland Nursery Sales in 1978.

NAME Chicago Peace

RATING ARS 8.3; Gold Medal Portland, 1961. Deserves to have been much more highly honored.

TYPE Hybrid Tea

ORIGIN Introduced by Conard Pyle Co. in 1962. A sport of the famous Peace Rose discovered among a planting of Peace in the rose garden at Cantigny Museum, near Chicago.

HEIGHT 5 feet; upright, bushy habit.

FRAGRANCE Slight, same as Peace Rose.

DESCRIPTION Large, double blooms are up to 5½ inches across. All the colors of Peace are accentuated by deeper coloring in Chicago Peace—a deeper yellow basic color and deeper pink highlights—contrasting magnificently against large, glossy, leathery, dark green leaves. A true connoisseur's rose considered to be a distinct improvement over the original Peace Rose largely because of its stronger color tones. Plants are vigorous, the blooms are exhibition quality, and flower arrangers adore the swirled, high-centered, mature bud stage as sweetheart roses.

NAME Christian Dior

RATING ARS 7.7; AARS Award, 1962; Gold Medal Geneva, 1958.

TYPE Hybrid Tea

ORIGIN Hybridized by the House of Meilland, in France, and introduced in the United States through Conard Pyle Co. in 1958. A cross between a seedling of Independence x Happiness and a seedling of Peace x Happiness.

HEIGHT 5 feet; bushy, erect habit.

FRAGRANCE Surprisingly slight considering it was named for the head of the House of Dior, famous for fashion and perfume.

DESCRIPTION What this rose lacks in perfume it more than makes up for in quality of its flowers, regarded as one of the best for exhibition. Blood red blooms are up to 4½ inches across, made up of fifty-five petals with a heavy, velvety texture. Glossy, leathery, dark green leaves are a perfect background, though susceptible to mildew. Long-lasting as a cut flower, this is one of America's top-selling roses, appealing to everyone's sense of what a red-red rose should look like.

NAME Chrysler Imperial

RATING ARS 8.3; AARS Award, 1953; Gold Medal Portland, 1951 and other international awards.

TYPE Hybrid Tea

ORIGIN Hybridized by Lammerts, California, and introduced through Germain's in 1952. A cross between Charlotte Armstrong and Mirandy.

HEIGHT Up to 5 feet; upright, bushy habit. May need heavy pruning to keep it compact.

FRAGRANCE Strong and spicy, reminiscent of cloves.

DESCRIPTION One of America's top-selling roses on account of its classic form and heavy substance. The large flowers measure up to 5 inches across, colored a dusky, deep red that darkens with age. The dark green leaves are prone to mildew in humid climates, but otherwise its bloom production is heavy, with flowers that win prizes at shows and are beloved by arrangers.

NAME Color Magic

RATING ARS 8.0; AARS Award, 1978.

TYPE Hybrid Tea

ORIGIN Introduced by Jackson & Perkins in 1978. A cross between Spellbinder and an unnamed seedling.

HEIGHT 5 feet; bushy, upright habit.

FRAGRANCE Slight.

DESCRIPTION An excellent cut flower and show rose. The ivory-pink, 6- to 7-inch double blooms darken to a deep rose color with age. Leaves are glossy, dark green. Vigorous, disease-resistant plants. In cold climates it may need extra winter protection by mounding soil up around the main stems, or heavy mulching after the ground has frozen.

NAME Command Performance

RATING ARS 7.2; AARS Award, 1971.

TYPE Hybrid Tea

ORIGIN Hybridized by Robert V. Lindquist of California, and introduced in 1970. A cross between Tropicana and Hawaii.

HEIGHT 5 to 6 feet; upright, slender habit kept low by pruning.

FRAGRANCE Heavy, intoxicating aroma.

DESCRIPTION Superb, semi-double, 3- to 4-inch orange-red blooms flower from early summer to fall frost, though hot, humid weather puts it under temporary stress. The dark green, leathery leaves are susceptible to mildew, which accounts for its relatively low ARS rating, but its flowers are sensational and it is outstanding for garden display. Flower arrangers, too, admire its shapely, scented blooms.

NAME Confidence

RATING ARS 8.0; Gold Medal Bagatelle, 1951.

TYPE Hybrid Tea

ORIGIN Introduced by the House of Meilland, France, through the Conard Pyle Co. A cross between Peace and Michele Meilland.

HEIGHT Up to 4 feet; upright, bushy habit.

FRAGRANCE Delightful, heavy, satisfying fragrance.

DESCRIPTION The creamy pastel tones of pink, yellow, and peach blend together exquisitely, producing a beautiful contrast to the dark green, leathery leaves. The large, individual flowers are high-centered, up to 5 inches across. Good for garden display on account of its heavy bloom production, also a good show rose and valued by flower arrangers for the high-centered flowers.

NAME Dolly Parton

RATING ARS 7.4.

TYPE Hybrid Tea

ORIGIN Hybridized by Joseph Winchel and introduced by Conard Pyle Co. in 1984. A cross between Fragrant Cloud and Oklahoma.

HEIGHT Up to 5 feet; erect, vigorous habit.

FRAGRANCE Exceptionally heavy fragrance. The rich, fruity, almost intoxicating fragrance is noticeable even before the flowers are fully open.

DESCRIPTION One of the largest flowering hybrid tea roses of all time. Like its namesake, the flamboyant, cheerful country and western singer, the Dolly Parton Rose is bright, colorful, full-formed, and beautiful—a star that commands attention. Individual flowers measure up to 6 inches across, are fully double, and are a luminous orange-red. Thick canes support the heavy, heady blooms without bending.

NAME Double Delight

RATING ARS 8.8; AARS Award, 1977; Gold Medal Rome, 1976 and other international awards.

TYPE Hybrid Tea

ORIGIN Introduced in 1977 by Armstrong Nurseries, California. A cross between Granada and Garden Party.

HEIGHT 4 feet; spreading, bushy habit. Climbing Double Delight, a sport, grows much taller.

FRAGRANCE Heavy, spicy fragrance.

DESCRIPTION The profilic, double, bicolored flowers are up to 6 inches across. They are a glorious combination of creamy white and red petals, with the creamy white ones concentrated towards the center. It is an absolutely uplifting sight to see these in the garden, and also to find they have such a heavenly fragrance! The leaves are a perfect contrast—dark green, disease-resistant, and glossy. Plants are vigorous, though somewhat tender. An incredibly beautiful color combination in a garden display, but also a favorite among flower arrangers. The climber, too, is sensational though rather a shy bloomer compared to other climbers.

NAME Electron

RATING ARS 7.7; AARS Award, 1973 and other international awards.

TYPE Hybrid Tea

ORIGIN Introduced in 1970 by the House of McGredy, New Zealand. A cross between Paddy McGredy and Prima Ballerina.

HEIGHT Up to 4 feet; bushy, erect habit.

FRAGRANCE Delightfully fragrant.

DESCRIPTION Long-lasting, glowing, rose-pink, double blooms range from 3 to 5 inches across. The ideal pink rose that photographers like to work with. Buds open slowly into spectacular flowers of classic form. Lush, dark green leaves cover the plant to the ground. Remarkably heat- and disease-resistant. Very free flowering even under unfavorable conditions. An exceptional rose for both garden display and flower arrangements.

NAME Fragrant Cloud

RATING ARS 8.0; Gold Medal from the National Rose Society, 1963 and other national awards.

TYPE Hybrid Tea

ORIGIN Introduced in 1968 by the House of Tantau, West Germany. A cross between Prima Ballerina and an unnamed seedling.

HEIGHT 5 feet; upright, branching habit.

FRAGRANCE One of the all-time best roses for heavy fragrance. Just a few blooms will fill a room with their aroma.

DESCRIPTION Long-stemmed, 5-inch, double, shapely, coral-red flowers appear singly or in clusters of two's. Dark, glossy leaves help accentuate the beauty of the blossoms. Plants are vigorous and disease-resistant. Excellent for exhibition and highly prized by flower arrangers not only for their intense tea-rose perfume, but also for its shape at all stages of development, from bud to petal drop.

NAME Garden Party

RATING ARS 8.6; AARS Award, 1960; Gold Medal Bagatelle, 1959.

TYPE Hybrid Tea

ORIGIN Introduced in 1959 by Armstrong Roses, California. A cross between Charlotte Armstrong and Peace.

HEIGHT 4 feet; upright, branching habit.

FRAGRANCE Slight.

DESCRIPTION Double, high-centered, ivory buds have a blush of pink on the petal margins. These open into 4- to 5-inch creamy, ivory blossoms on long, strong stems. Luxurious, semi-glossy, dark green leaves are a perfect background to the profuse quantities of flowers. Good winter hardiness and disease resistance, except for mildew. A top exhibition rose and a popular cut flower.

NAME Honor

RATING ARS 8.0; AARS Award, 1980 and other awards.

TYPE Hybrid Tea

ORIGIN Introduced in 1980 by Jackson & Perkins, Oregon. Parents unknown.

HEIGHT 4 feet; upright, slender habit.

FRAGRANCE Light.

DESCRIPTION Pure white, double, 5-inch blooms are held erect on strong stems. Plants are vigorous and disease-resistant, flowering continuously throughout the growing season, even during hot weather. Originally introduced as a threesome with Love (red) and Cherish (coral pink), all developed by the same breeder. Good for garden display on account of its prolific blooming; also an exquisite cut flower.

NAME King's Ransom

RATING ARS 6.7; AARS Award, 1962.

TYPE Hybrid Tea

ORIGIN Introduced in 1962 by Jackson & Perkins, Oregon. A cross between Golden Masterpiece and Lydia.

HEIGHT 3 to 4 feet; erect habit.

FRAGRANCE Moderate.

DESCRIPTION Large, golden yellow, handsome flowers up to 6 inches across, have high centers and prominent darker yellow petal veins. Lower petals have a tendency to curl under and end in a tapered point, giving some of the flowers a distinct spidery effect. Dark green, leathery, glossy leaves accentuate the brilliant colored blossoms. Plants are vigorous, producing long, strong, flowering stems excellent for cutting. Generally considered to be greatly underrated by the ARS rating system.

NAME Medallion

RATING ARS 7.6; AARS Award, 1973.

TYPE Hybrid Tea

ORIGIN Introduced in 1973 by Jackson & Perkins, Oregon. A cross between South Seas and King's Ransom.

HEIGHT 4 feet; bushy, branching habit.

FRAGRANCE Moderate, fruity aroma reminiscent of ripe apples.

DESCRIPTION Long, graceful, buff apricot buds have a hint of pink in their coloration. The dramatic flowers unfold into gigantic, double, pale apricot specimens, up to 8 inches across, borne singly on long, strong stems. Flower color tends to be pinkish in cooler climates, more apricot in warmer areas. Leaves are large and dark green. Plants are vigorous, hardy, and disease-resistant. Frequently produces its best display in autumn. Useful as a hedge or screen. A popular rose for making fresh bouquets on account of the spectacular flower size.

NAME Miss All-American Beauty

RATING ARS 8.7; AARS Award, 1968.

TYPE Hybrid Tea

ORIGIN Introduced by the House of Meilland, France, in 1967. A cross between Chrysler Imperial and Karl Herbst.

HEIGHT Up to 4 feet; bushy habit. Climbing Miss All-American Beauty grows much taller.

FRAGRANCE Moderate to strong tea-rose fragrance.

DESCRIPTION Big, bold, perfectly-shaped, hot pink flowers make this one of the best pink hybrid teas. Retains its rich, deep pink color throughout the flowering cycle, from bud formation, to the opening of the petals, to the disintegration of the flower parts. Individual flowers can measure up to 5 inches across, and are freely produced on hardy, disease-resistant plants. A popular choice for mass planting in beds. A good cut flower—one of America's top-selling roses.

NAME Mister Lincoln

RATING ARS 8.7; AARS Award, 1965.

TYPE Hybrid Tea

ORIGIN Introduced in 1963, and hybridized by Swim & Weeks, California, through the Conard Pyle Co., Pennsylvania. A cross between Chrysler Imperial and Charles Mallerin.

HEIGHT Usually over 4 feet; upright, vigorous, bushy habit.

FRAGRANCE Heavy. One of the best for filling a room with the perfume of roses.

DESCRIPTION Beautiful, long, pointed buds open to dazzling deep red blooms up to 6 inches across. Plants are free-flowering over a long period. Flowers have a velvety texture and the dark red coloring much admired by flower arrangers. The color holds true even in high temperatures. Large, dark green, leathery leaves are a perfect foil to the flowers. Top exhibition quality.

NAME Olympiad

RATING ARS 8.1; AARS Award; 1984.

TYPE Hybrid Tea

ORIGIN Hybridized by the House of McGredy, New Zealand, and introduced in 1984 by Armstrong Nurseries, California.

HEIGHT 3 to 5 feet; bushy, upright habit.

FRAGRANCE Slight.

DESCRIPTION The official rose of the 1984 Olympic Games, and the only deep red rose to win an AARS Award since Mister Lincoln. Large, exhibition quality flowers up to 5 inches across are produced in great profusion on long, strong stems. The vigorous plants are hardy, disease-resistant, and covered with medium green leaves, making Olympiad a popular choice for mass plantings.

NAME Oregold

RATING ARS 7.5; AARS Award, 1975.

TYPE Hybrid Tea

ORIGIN Hybridized by the House of Tantau, West Germany, and introduced in 1975 by Jackson & Perkins, Oregon. A cross between Piccadilly and Konigin der Rosen.

HEIGHT 4 feet; upright, bushy habit.

FRAGRANCE Light, pleasant, tea-rose fragrance.

DESCRIPTION One of the most popular yellow roses because of its extra large flowers, which are a deep golden yellow, up to 6 inches across, and borne singly on long, strong, thorny stems. Profilic repeat bloomer that doesn't fade. The dark green, glossy foliage is a perfect contrast for the bright flowers. Plants are vigorous and disease-resistant, though not reliably hardy where summers are hot and humid and winters are subjected to prolonged freezing periods. Top exhibition quality; the high-pointed flowers are also prized for cutting.

NAME Paradise

RATING ARS 8.5; AARS Award, 1979.

TYPE Hybrid Tea

ORIGIN Hybridized by the House of Weeks, California, and introduced in 1979 by Conard Pyle Co., Pennsylvania. A cross between Swarthmore and an unnamed seedling.

HEIGHT Up to 4 feet; bushy, compact habit.

FRAGRANCE Lightly scented.

DESCRIPTION When the House of Meilland, in France, introduced Princess de Monaco it caused a sensation among flower arrangers who loved its delicate ivory white petals with a blush of pink along the petal tips. Then along came Paradise, with deeper bicolor hues—silvery lavender edged in deep pink. The two make an incredible color combination in a floral arrangement. Individual flowers of Paradise measure up to 5 inches across, and hold their form and color well. Plants are vigorous, disease-resistant, and prolific bloomers.

NAME Pascali

RATING ARS 8.4; AARS Award, 1969 and other awards.

TYPE Hybrid Tea

ORIGIN Hybridized by the House of Dickson, Northern Ireland, and introduced in 1968 by Armstrong Nurseries, California.

HEIGHT 4 feet and more; bushy, upright habit.

FRAGRANCE Slight.

DESCRIPTION Strong, vigorous canes bear glistening, creamy white flowers of medium size, 3 to 4 inches across. The high-centered, double blooms are borne in profusion. An exceptional white rose since it is reasonably free of mildew and holds its color well even under adverse conditions. Good for exhibition and cutting. Makes a beautiful tree-form standard and container patio plant by pruning.

NAME Peace

RATING ARS 8.5; AARS Award, 1946 and many other international awards.

TYPE Hybrid Tea

ORIGIN Hybridized by the House of Meilland, France, and introduced in 1945 by Conard Pyle Co., Pennsylvania (see "The Story of Peace Rose," page 18). Produced by a complex cross involving Margaret McGredy Rose as one parent and a seedling produced from other crosses as the other parent.

HEIGHT Up to 5 feet; erect, bushy habit. Climbing Peace grows taller.

FRAGRANCE Slight tea-rose fragrance.

DESCRIPTION Probably the world's best-known rose and the parent of many other fine roses since its introduction, including Pink Peace and Chicago Peace. The original Peace Rose produces immense blooms up to 6 inches across, with pale yellow petals flushed with deep pink or magenta at the petal tips. Plants are vigorous, hardy, and disease-resistant, growing stiff canes covered with glossy, dark green leaves. An excellent rose to plant as a single specimen. Its beautiful blooms are exhibition quality and prized by floral arrangers from its mature bud stage to petal drop.

NAME Perfume Delight

RATING ARS 7.7; AARS Award, 1974.

TYPE Hybrid Tea

ORIGIN Hybridized by the House of Weeks, California, and introduced in 1973 by Conard Pyle Co., Pennsylvania. Complex crosses that include Chrysler Imperial and Peace Roses in its parentage.

HEIGHT Up to 4 feet; bushy, upright habit.

FRAGRANCE Heavy, spicy, old-fashioned rose scent.

DESCRIPTION Rich, deep pink, double blooms with a satinlike sheen to the petals, grow up to 5 inches across, borne erect on long, strong stems. Flowers continuously throughout the growing season, though heaviest bloom production is in spring and autumn. Large, leathery, dull, olive-green leaves enhance the flowering display. Excellent show rose. Good for cutting—especially in the mature bud stage with their long, pointed shape.

NAME Pink Peace

RATING ARS 7.7; AARS Award, 1974; Gold Medal at Geneva and Rome, 1959.

TYPE Hybrid Tea

ORIGIN Hybridized by the House of Meilland, France, and introduced in 1959 by Conard Pyle Co., Pennsylvania. A cross between Peace x Monique and Peace x Mrs. John Laing.

HEIGHT 4 feet and more; upright, bushy habit.

FRAGRANCE Intense old rose fragrance, much stronger than the original Peace Rose.

DESCRIPTION Identical to the original Peace Rose in shape and size of bloom (up to 6 inches across), but with a sensational, uniform, deep rose coloring and heavenly fragrance to match. Vigorous plants are repeat blooming, though the large, blue-green, leathery leaves are susceptible to mildew. An attractive, show quality rose that can be used alone as a lawn highlight, massed in a bed, or planted in a line to create a hedge.

NAME Pristine

RATING ARS 8.0.

TYPE Hybrid Tea

ORIGIN Hybridized by Bill Warriner and introduced by Jackson & Perkins, Oregon, in 1978. A cross between White Masterpiece and First Prize.

HEIGHT Up to 4 feet; upright, slightly spreading habit.

FRAGRANCE Slight.

DESCRIPTION Large, high-pointed ivory white flowers and the look of fine porcelain characterize this show quality rose. A touch of soft pink colors the petal edges. The hardy, disease-resistant plants produce glossy, dark, reddish green leaves. Very popular among flower arrangers who use it predominently in the mature bud stage.

NAME Red Masterpiece

RATING ARS 7.2.

TYPE Hybrid Tea

ORIGIN Hybridized by Jack Warriner and introduced in 1974 by Jackson & Perkins, Oregon. A cross between Siren x Chrysler Imperial and Carrousel x Chrysler Imperial.

HEIGHT Up to 4 feet; bushy, upright habit.

FRAGRANCE Heavy, old-fashioned rose scent.

DESCRIPTION Long, sturdy stems hold classic, dark red, double blooms measuring up to 6 inches across. Would be much higher rated by the American Rose Society if it were not so prone to mildew. Nevertheless, plants are vigorous, the flowers hold their gorgeous red coloring even under adverse conditions, and the dark, leathery, green leaves complement the flowers, which are of exhibition quality and admired by flower arrangers who especially value the mature bud stage for use as sweetheart roses.

NAME Royal Highness

RATING ARS 8.5; AARS Award, 1963 and other awards.

TYPE Hybrid Tea

ORIGIN Hybridized by Swim & Weeks, California, and introduced in 1962 by Conard Pyle Co., Pennsylvania. A cross between Virgo and Peace.

HEIGHT 3 to 4 feet; low, bushy habit.

FRAGRANCE Pleasant, heavy fragrance.

DESCRIPTION Long, pointed buds open to double, soft pink blooms up to 5$\frac{1}{2}$ inches across on long, strong stems. Leathery, dark green leaves are an excellent contrast to the light coloring of the flowers. The delicate pink coloring and classic, high-centered shape of the flowers make this a popular rose to paint, to photograph, and to write poetry about. Exhibition quality; excellent for cutting. A rose with enduring popularity.

NAME Sutter' s Gold

RATING ARS 6.9; AARS Award, 1950 and other international awards.

TYPE Hybrid Tea

ORIGIN Hybridized by Herbert H. Swim, California, and introduced by Armstrong Nurseries, California, in 1950. A cross between Charlotte Armstrong and Signora.

HEIGHT Up to 4 feet; erect, spreading, compact habit. Climbing Sutter's Gold grows much taller.

FRAGRANCE Heavy, fruity scent. Winner of the James Alexander Gamble Award for rose fragrance in 1966.

DESCRIPTION Beautiful, high-centered, 4- to 5-inch double blooms are golden yellow, with a slight tinge of salmon-pink at the petal edges. Vigorous plants are disease-resistant, have dark, glossy green, leathery leaves. Prefers cool weather. In its half-open bud stage it makes a particularly fine cut flower.

Right: Just Joey is a highly fragrant hybrid tea rose with large, double, buff-orange blooms.

NAME Tropicana

RATING ARS 8.4; AARS Award, 1963 and other awards.

TYPE Hybrid Tea

ORIGIN Hybridized by the House of Tantau, West Germany, and introduced in 1960 by Jackson & Perkins, Oregon.

HEIGHT 4 to 5 feet; upright, spreading habit. Climbing Tropicana grows much taller.

FRAGRANCE Heavy, fruity aroma.

DESCRIPTION Considered the best of the orange-red roses. The coral-orange coloring is almost fluorescent, while the double, 4- to 5-inch blooms are exquisitely shaped. Plants are vigorous though prone to mildew. Glossy, leathery, dark green leaves help to accentuate the flowers. Prolific blooming under a wide range of climatic conditions. Exhibition quality and good for cutting.

NAME White Masterpiece

RATING ARS 7.6.

TYPE Hybrid Tea

ORIGIN Hybridized by Eugene Boerner and introduced in 1969 by Jackson & Perkins, Oregon. A cross between two unnamed seedlings of unknown origin.

HEIGHT Up to 4 feet; upright, spreading habit.

FRAGRANCE Light and sweet.

DESCRIPTION Exquisite flower form and large size. The double, pure white blooms measure up to 6 inches across. Considered the best of the pure white hybrid tea roses. Blooms throughout the growing season. Vigorous plants are disease-resistant and can adapt to a wide range of climatic conditions. Glossy, dark green leaves and strong-flowering stems. A superb cut flower and top exhibition quality rose.

FLORIBUNDA ROSES

A modern group of roses more recent than the large-flowered hybrid teas, developed from crossing hybrid tea roses with old-fashioned polyantha (shrub) roses. Floribundas have smaller individual flowers than hybrid teas, but the flowers generally form a big, bold cluster. They are especially valuable for massing in beds and borders where a bold splash of color is needed. The more compact varieties are sometimes grown in tubs for decorating patios and decks. Floribundas are cherished by flower arrangers for informal arrangements and where a stunning mass of color is wanted. A single flowering stem of floribundas will make an instant bouquet.

Below is the floribunda rose, Showbiz.

NAME Accent

RATING ARS 7.0.

TYPE Floribunda

ORIGIN Hybridized by Bill Warriner and introduced in 1977 by Jackson & Perkins, Oregon. A cross between Marlena and an unnamed seedling.

HEIGHT 3 to 4 feet; bushy, compact growth.

FRAGRANCE Slightly fragrant.

DESCRIPTION Double, cardinal red flowers measure up to 2½ inches across and are grouped together in bold clusters, each of which makes an instant bouquet. Small, dark green, leathery leaves. Outstanding for mass bedding and to highlight a mixed shrub or perennial border.

NAME Betty Prior

RATING ARS 8.5; Gold Medal, National Rose Society of Great Britain, 1933.

TYPE Floribunda

ORIGIN Hybridized by Betty Prior, Great Britain, and introduced in 1935 by Jackson & Perkins, then headquartered in New York State. A cross between Kirsten Poulsen and an unnamed seedling.

HEIGHT 4 feet; bushy habit.

FRAGRANCE Very slight.

DESCRIPTION A wonderful, vigorous, free-flowering, single rose that has an appealing, old-fashioned look about it. The carmine-pink flowers have just five petals, and measure up to 3 inches across. They are borne in generous clusters of up to thirty flowers per cluster, in such profusion that they can almost completely hide the foliage. Probably the most prolific flowering floribunda ever developed. Plants are strong growers, hardy, disease-resistant, and display leathery, dark green leaves. Though flowering occurs all at one time—in early summer—Betty Prior makes a wonderful highlight used alone, but is most attractive when planted as a short hedge.

NAME Cathedral

RATING ARS 7.4; AARS Award, 1976 and other awards.

TYPE Floribunda

ORIGIN Hybridized by the House of McGredy, New Zealand, in 1975. A cross between Little Darling x Goldilocks and Irish Mist.

HEIGHT 4 feet; compact, bushy habit.

FRAGRANCE Slight.

DESCRIPTION Apricot to salmon double blooms measure up to 5 inches across, and are borne in small clusters on short stems. Almost a grandiflora in appearance. The glossy, coppery green leaves are disease-resistant, particularly to mildew. An elegant cut flower and an excellent exhibition rose.

NAME Charisma

RATING ARS 8.0; AARS Award, 1978.

TYPE Floribunda

ORIGIN Hybridized by E. G. Hill Co., Indiana, and introduced in 1977 by Conard Pyle Co., Pennsylvania. A cross between Gemini and Zorina.

HEIGHT 4 feet; bushy, erect habit.

FRAGRANCE Slight.

DESCRIPTION Oval buds open into double blooms, 2 to 2½ inches across, with scarlet petal tips. Color intensifies with age. Its glossy, leathery, green leaves, abundant, continuous flowering, and compact growth habit make this an excellent bedding rose. The generous flower clusters can be picked as an instant bouquet. The color is heightened under indoor lighting.

NAME Fashion

RATING ARS 7.7; AARS Award, 1950 and other international awards.

TYPE Floribunda

ORIGIN Hybridized by Gene Boerner and introduced in 1949 by Jackson & Perkins, at that time headquartered in New York State. A cross between Pinocchio and Crimson Glory.

HEIGHT 4 feet; vigorous, bushy habit. Climbing Fashion grows much taller.

FRAGRANCE Moderate.

DESCRIPTION Beautiful coral-peach, double blooms, measuring 3 to 3½ inches across, are borne in tight clusters. Attractive, glossy, bronze-green foliage. A profuse bloomer, Fashion is disease-resistant and holds color well even in hot weather. Outstanding for garden display and bedding. Combines well with yellow, pink, and lavender floribundas.

NAME Fire King

RATING ARS 7.5; AARS Award, 1960.

TYPE Floribunda

ORIGIN Hybridized by the House of Meilland, France, and introduced in 1958 by Conard Pyle Co., Pennsylvania. A cross between Moulin Rouge and Fashion.

HEIGHT Up to 4 feet; upright, bushy habit.

FRAGRANCE Musky fragrance.

DESCRIPTION Fiery scarlet, double flowers up to 3 inches across, are borne in clusters. Plants are vigorous, have dark green, leathery leaves. Especially good for garden display where a mass of red is desirable. Mix with white and yellow floribundas for beautiful border.

NAME First Edition

RATING ARS 8.4; AARS Award, 1977.

TYPE Floribunda

ORIGIN Hybridized by the House of Delbard, France, and introduced in 1976 by Conard Pyle Co., Pennsylvania. Complicated crosses involving Zambra, Orleans x Goldilocks, and an Orange Triumph seedling x Florada.

HEIGHT 4 feet; erect, bushy habit.

FRAGRANCE Slight.

DESCRIPTION Continuous flowering, vigorous plants are highly resistant to both mildew and black spot diseases. Flowers are semi-double, and measure 2½ inches across. They have a brilliant coral color, shading to orange. Color is more vibrant during cool weather. Glossy, leathery, olive-green foliage helps to make this an excellent rose to use as a low hedge or massed in a border. One of the all-time great floribunda roses—useful as a container plant; it is exhibition quality and good for cutting.

NAME French Lace

RATING ARS 7.8; AARS Award, 1982.

TYPE Floribunda

ORIGIN Hybridized by Bill Warriner and introduced in 1982 by Jackson & Perkins, Oregon. A cross between Dr. A. J. Verhage and Bridal Pink.

HEIGHT 4 feet; bushy, erect habit.

FRAGRANCE Slight.

DESCRIPTION Lovely, 3- to 4-inch double, ivory white blooms are delicately flushed with peach, and produce up to twelve flowers to a cluster. Vigorous plants are disease-resistant, and produce glossy, leathery, dark green foliage that helps to display the flowers to perfection. Perpetual flowering from spring until fall frost, with heaviest blooming occurring in cool weather. The exhibition quality blooms make exquisite cut flowers. Good for garden display, too. Worth growing in pots. If you have room for only one white rose, this is it.

NAME Gene Boerner

RATING ARS 8.7; AARS Award, 1969.

TYPE Floribunda

ORIGIN Hybridized by Gene Boerner and introduced in 1969 by Jackson & Perkins, Oregon. A cross between Ginger and Ma Perkins x Garnette Supreme.

HEIGHT 5 feet; bushy, vigorous, erect habit.

FRAGRANCE Slight tea scent.

DESCRIPTION Oval buds with high centers turn into true pink, double blooms, 3 to 3½ inches across, borne in clusters on long, strong stems. Glossy, green leaves are a good complement to the flowers. Disease-resistant plants grow a little taller than most floribundas but the flowers are exhibition quality and greatly admired by flower arrangers not only for their lovely color but also for their elegant shape in the mature bud stage.

NAME Iceberg

RATING ARS 8.9; Gold Medal from the National Rose Society of Great Britain, 1958 and other awards.

TYPE Floribunda

ORIGIN Hybridized by the House of Kordes, West Germany and introduced in 1958. A cross between Robin Hood and Virgo.

HEIGHT 6 to 8 feet; tall, rounded, bushy habit. Climbing Iceberg grows to 10 feet and higher.

FRAGRANCE Sweetly scented.

DESCRIPTION One of the most popular white-flowering floribundas where a torrent of blossoms is desired. An avalanche of pure white double blooms, up to 4 inches across, occurs during the cool weather of early summer and autumn, though the plant is rarely without flowers except when dormant. The huge flower clusters contrast well against the shiny green leaves. Plants are hardy, disease-resistant, and almost thornless. Iceberg needs room to spread its billowing canes, and Climbing Iceberg needs strong support for its heavy mantle of blooms. An essential component of the garden where a "wedding theme" or an "all-white" emphasis is desired. Truly, an incredible sight when in full flower.

NAME Impatient

RATING ARS 8.0; AARS Award, 1984.

TYPE Floribunda

ORIGIN Hybridized by Bill Warriner and introduced in 1984 by Jackson & Perkins, Oregon.

HEIGHT 3 to 4 feet; upright, bushy habit.

FRAGRANCE Slight.

DESCRIPTION The only purpose in life this vigorous rose seems to have is to flower its head off. Semi-double, brilliant, orange-red flowers measure 3 inches across, and are clustered together in huge trusses. Any one flower cluster makes a big bouquet. New foliage growth is mahogany, turning to dark green. Flowers heavily in early summer and again in autumn during cool weather. An outstanding name for this extremely free-flowering floribunda that is now recognized as perhaps the very best for mass bedding. Combines extremely well with yellow roses, such as Sunsprite.

NAME Ivory Fashion

RATING ARS 8.7; AARS Award, 1959.

TYPE Floribunda

ORIGIN Hybridized by Gene Boerner and introduced by Jackson & Perkins, Oregon, in 1958. A cross between Sonata and Fashion.

HEIGHT 3 feet; upright habit.

FRAGRANCE Moderate.

DESCRIPTION Ivory white, semi-double, flat blooms measure up to $4^{1}/_{2}$ inches across, and are borne in large clusters. Leathery, medium green leaves. Vigorous plants are disease-resistant and free-flowering. Long-lasting as a cut flower as only one stem will form a bouquet. Useful for massing in beds and for creating a low hedge.

NAME Marina

RATING ARS 8.0; AARS Award, 1981.

TYPE Floribunda

ORIGIN Hybridized by the House of Kordes, West Germany. A cross between Color Wonder and an unnamed seedling.

HEIGHT 4 feet; upright habit.

FRAGRANCE Lightly scented.

DESCRIPTION Lovely orange flowers are yellow at the petal center, beautifully double. Buds are long and pointed—exquisite for flower arranging. They are often sold as sweetheart roses in the mature bud stage. Foliage is glossy, dark, and leathery. Generous bloom production throughout the season, the flowers grouped in typical floribunda-type clusters.

NAME Showbiz

RATING ARS 8.1; AARS Award, 1985.

TYPE Floribunda

ORIGIN Hybridized by the House of Tantau, West Germany, in 1981. Parentage not disclosed, but obviously a cross involving floribunda roses.

HEIGHT 4 feet; bushy habit.

FRAGRANCE None.

DESCRIPTION Brilliant, medium red, double flowers grow up to $2\frac{1}{2}$ inches across, and are borne in large clusters throughout the growing season, with a particularly strong flush of color in early summer and again in autumn during cool weather. An extravagant flower show on compact, tidy plants, excellent for mass bedding. Dark green, semi-glossy foliage is a perfect background to its spectacular flower clusters.

NAME Simplicity

RATING ARS 8.3; Gold Medal New Zealand, 1976.

TYPE Floribunda, sometimes listed as a shrub or hedge rose.

ORIGIN Hybridized by Bill Warriner and introduced through Jackson & Perkins, Oregon, in 1976. A cross between Iceberg and an unnamed seedling.

HEIGHT Upright, bushy habit; 4 to 5 feet high.

FRAGRANCE Slightly fragrant.

DESCRIPTION Simplicity has become one of the biggest-selling roses of all time, largely due to its value as a hedge rose and the desire among gardeners to use it for screening, edging driveways, and planting as a "living fence". Plants are highly disease-resistant and perpetual blooming, displaying masses of lovely, shell pink, semi-double, 4-inch flowers, grouped in clusters of four or five blooms. Very similar in appearance to Carefree Beauty, a perpetual-flowering hedge rose with good disease resistance, introduced by Conard Pyle Co., Pennsylvania.

NAME Sunsprite

RATING ARS 8.0; Gold Medal Baden Baden, 1972.

TYPE Floribunda

ORIGIN Hybridized by the House of Kordes, West Germany, in 1977 and introduced by Jackson & Perkins, Oregon. A cross between Spanish Sun and an unnamed seedling.

HEIGHT 3 to 4 feet; upright habit.

FRAGRANCE Moderate to strong.

DESCRIPTION Deep yellow, double, cupped blooms are borne in dense clusters, each flower up to 3 inches across. The deep green foliage is a good contrast to the flowers, which are fade-resistant and flower continuously from early summer to fall frosts, with heaviest blooming occurring during cool weather. Plants are vigorous and are good for massed bedding displays. One of the best yellow floribundas, Sunsprite makes a particularly good companion to orange, scarlet, and red floribunda roses.

NAME Vogue

RATING ARS 7.5; AARS Award, 1952 and other awards.

TYPE Floribunda

ORIGIN Hybridized by Gene Boerner and introduced by Jackson & Perkins, Oregon. A cross between Pinocchio and Crimson Glory.

HEIGHT 3 to 4 feet; upright, bushy habit.

FRAGRANCE Pleasant, medium fragrance.

DESCRIPTION Cherry-coral, high-centered, double flowers grow to $3^{1}/_{2}$ to $4^{1}/_{2}$ inches across and are borne in large clusters. Vigorous plants produce attractive, glossy green leaves. Mostly used for bedding because of its capacity to flower so freely in spring and autumn during cool weather. One spray of flowers can make a bouquet. Looks especially good planted in combination with a deep red floribunda, such as Fire King or Impatient.

GRANDIFLORA ROSES

This class was established in the 1950s especially for the rose variety Queen Elizabeth. Grandiflora roses have large blooms like hybrid teas, but they are borne in clusters, like floribundas. In most respects, grandiflora roses should be treated like hybrid teas and used as mass plantings in beds and borders. Since the introduction of Queen Elizabeth, a number of other garden worthy roses have been classified as grandifloras.

Below is the grandiflora rose, Love.

NAME Arizona

RATING ARS 6.2; AARS Award, 1975.

TYPE Grandiflora

ORIGIN Hybridized by the House of Weeks, California, and introduced in 1975 by Conard Pyle Co., Pennsylvania. A cross involving Golden Scepter and Golden Rapture.

HEIGHT 4 to 6 feet; tall, bushy habit.

FRAGRANCE Strong.

DESCRIPTION Double, golden bronze blooms measure up to 4 inches across, and are borne singly and in clusters of two or three on long, thorny stems. Semi-glossy, leathery, bronze-green foliage is disease-resistant. Popular in mass plantings and as a hedging rose. Excellent cut flower.

NAME Love

RATING ARS 7.5; AARS Award, 1980.

TYPE Grandiflora

ORIGIN Hybridized by Bill Warriner and introduced in 1980 by Jackson & Perkins, Oregon. A cross between Redgold and an unnamed seedling.

HEIGHT 3 to 4 feet; bushy, upright habit.

FRAGRANCE Light, spicy fragrance.

DESCRIPTION Plump, pointed buds unfold into magnificent bright red, bicolored double blooms with high centers and silvery white undersides. Flowers are up to 3⅓ inches across with recurved petals. Seen from above the flowers look all red; from the side or below they show their bicolored effect to perfection. Several blooms may appear in a cluster, contrasting against the medium green foliage. One of the best of all roses for cutting to create stunning arrangements. The blooms are also exhibition quality.

NAME Queen Elizabeth

RATING ARS 9.1; AARS Award, 1955 and other international awards.

TYPE Grandiflora

ORIGIN Hybridized by the House of Lammerts, California, and introduced in 1954 by Germain's Roses, California. A cross between Charlotte Armstrong and Floradora.

HEIGHT 4 to 6 feet; erect, bushy habit. Climbing Queen Elizabeth is much taller, growing up to 10 feet.

FRAGRANCE Moderately fragrant.

DESCRIPTION Profuse double, high-centered blooms are up to 4 inches across. Color is carmine, fading to pale pink. Flowers are borne singly and in clusters of up to five on long, almost thornless stems. Beautiful, dark green, glossy foliage. Plants are vigorous, hardy, and disease-resistant. A classic—the first of the grandiflora roses and still the highest rated. Makes an exceptional hedge, screen, or tall background planting because it blooms continuously. Admired by flower arrangers. One of the all-time top-selling roses in North America. Exhibition quality blooms repeatedly win prizes. One of the roses rated highest by the American Rose Society.

NAME Scarlet Knight

RATING ARS 7.8; AARS Award, 1968 and other awards.

TYPE Grandiflora

ORIGIN Hybridized by the House of Meilland, France, and introduced in 1966 by Conard Pyle Co., Pennsylvania. A cross between Happiness and Independence x Sutter's Gold.

HEIGHT Over 4 feet; upright, bushy habit.

FRAGRANCE Slight.

DESCRIPTION Double, brilliant scarlet blooms measuring 4 to 5 inches across, are borne in clusters of two or three blooms. Petals have a velvety texture. Leaves are leathery, glossy, and medium green. Plants are disease-resistant, and the blooms hold their color well. Good cut flower, especially mixed with pink roses; useful for bedding.

Left: The grandiflora class of hybrid roses was created specially for the variety Queen Elizabeth, which had the best attributes of both hybrid tea roses and floribundas— impressive large flowers like hybrid teas, borne in clusters like floribundas.
At left is the grandiflora rose, Love.

NAME Shreveport

RATING ARS 7.4; AARS Award, 1982.

TYPE Grandiflora

ORIGIN Hybridized by the House of Kordes, West Germany, and introduced in 1981 by Armstrong Roses, California. A cross between Zorina and Uwe Seeler.

HEIGHT 4 feet and more; tall, erect habit.

FRAGRANCE Mild tea fragrance.

DESCRIPTION Orange flowers are double, up to 4 inches across, and grow in clusters. Large, dark green, prickly leaves. Named in honor of the city where the American Rose Society is headquartered. Plants are vigorous and free-flowering; a popular cut flower because of its high, pointed shape in the mature bud stage.

NAME Sundowner

RATING ARS 7.5; AARS Award, 1979.

TYPE Grandiflora

ORIGIN Hybridized by the House of McGredy, New Zealand. A cross between Bond Street and Peer Gynt.

HEIGHT Up to 5 feet; tall, erect habit.

FRAGRANCE Strong, spicy aroma.

DESCRIPTION Golden orange, double blooms, $3^{1}/_{3}$ to 4 inches across are borne singly and occasionally in clusters of two or three, on long stems. Slightly recurved petals. Large, glossy, dark green leaves with copper overtones. Plants are vigorous, hardy, and resistant to blackspot but prone to mildew. Popular for cutting.

NAME White Lightenin'

RATING ARS 7.5; AARS Award, 1981.

TYPE Grandiflora

ORIGIN Hybridized and introduced by Armstrong Nurseries, California, in 1980. A cross between Angel Face and Misty.

HEIGHT 4 feet; upright, bushy habit.

FRAGRANCE Strong, citruslike scent.

DESCRIPTION Pointed, oval buds open out to clear white, double blossoms up to 4 inches across, in clusters. The petals are occasionally tinted at the edges with a blush of pink. Plants bloom profusely, the flowers contrasting beautifully with the glossy, dark green leaves. A sensational cut flower on account of its heavenly aroma and perfection at every stage of development, from bud formation to petal drop.

CLIMBING ROSES

This tall-growing group can include mutations of hybrid teas, floribundas, and miniatures, plus old-fashioned garden roses, species roses, and other groups. They are characterized by long, whiplike canes, which can climb unaided if the hooked thorns have branches and twigs of other woody plants to latch onto. However, in most garden situations, climbers are best grown up trellises, walls, and fences, in which case they need assistance, generally in the form of string or "twist ties" that can secure the cane firmly to a support.

Below is the climbing rose, Constance Spry.

NAME American Pillar

RATING Not yet rated by the American Rose Society.

TYPE Climber

ORIGIN Hybridized by Van Fleet and introduced in 1902 through Conard Pyle Co., Pennsylvania. A cross between *R. wichuraiana* (the Memorial Rose) and *R. setigera* (the Prairie Rose).

HEIGHT 15 to 20 feet; rambling habit.

FRAGRANCE None.

DESCRIPTION Carmine-pink, single flowers measuring up to 1 inch across, are grouped in large clusters 3 to 8 inches wide. One of the best climbing roses for covering arbors. Glossy, medium green, leathery leaves. Plants are vigorous, producing tremendous quantities of flowers over a three-week period in early summer. An especially good planting of American Pillar can be seen in June at Longwood Gardens, Pennsylvania, where they create a tunnel effect, supported on metal arches.

NAME Blaze, also called Improved Paul's Scarlet.

RATING ARS 7.9.

TYPE Climber

ORIGIN Introduced in 1932 by Jackson & Perkins, at that time headquartered in New York State. A cross between Paul's Scarlet and Gruss an Teplitz.

HEIGHT Up to 10 feet. Can be kept low and bushy by pruning, but its natural tendency is to grow long, pliable canes that can be trained vertically or horizontally.

FRAGRANCE Slight.

DESCRIPTION Strong-growing canes are covered with masses of cup-shaped, semi-double, bright red flowers measuring up to 2¼ inches across in early summer. One of America's top-selling roses. A well-grown specimen can produce so many flowers that they almost rub shoulder to shoulder, covering the foliage. Plants have good disease resistance, and display blue-green leaves. Prune by thinning out weak canes and leaving four strong canes, tied to a support during the winter. Especially good for training along fence rails, chain link fences, up trellises, and over arbors.

NAME City of York

RATING Not yet rated by the American Rose Society, though it won a Gold Medal Certificate from them in 1950.

TYPE Climber

ORIGIN Hybridized by the House of Tantau, West Germany, and introduced in 1945 by Conard Pyle Co., Pennsylvania. A cross between Dorothy Perkins and Professor Gnau.

HEIGHT Up to 10 feet; billowing, climbing habit.

FRAGRANCE None.

DESCRIPTION Probably named for its resemblance to old heraldic art associated with the House of York during the War of the Roses. Officially classified as a floribunda rose, but more often used as a climber because of its long canes and capacity to cover itself with an avalanche of flowers for several weeks in late spring. White, semi-double flower clusters measure up to 3 inches across. Dark green, glossy leaves look almost black when the flowers appear. Plants are vigorous, hardy, and appear to have a cast-iron constitution. Mostly used to decorate pergolas, arbors, and trellises. Always produces a stunning display along a high stone wall; an example can be seen in the rose garden at Longwood Gardens, Pennsylvania.

NAME Constance Spry

RATING Not yet rated by the American Rose Society.

TYPE Climber, officially classified as a shrub rose.

ORIGIN Hybridized by David Austin, England, and introduced in 1961. A cross between Belle Isis and Dainty Maid.

HEIGHT 5 to 10 feet; bushy habit, usually trained to climb.

FRAGRANCE Myrrhlike fragrance.

DESCRIPTION Has the appearance of an old-fashioned rose because the large, double, pink blooms are cupped and borne in clusters, with each flower measuring up to 5 inches across. Plants are vigorous, with dark green foliage. A favorite of flower arrangers because of the informal appearance of the flowers and their enchanting aroma. A good rose to decorate old stone walls, ornate ironwork, and picket fences.

NAME Don Juan

RATING ARS 8.3.

TYPE Climber

ORIGIN Hybridized by Michelle Malandrone, Italy, and introduced in 1958 by Jackson & Perkins, Oregon. A cross between a seedling of New Dawn and Detroiter.

HEIGHT 8 feet and more; upright, rambling habit.

FRAGRANCE Heavy.

DESCRIPTION A top-notch climber because of its unusually good fragrance and heavy bloom production. Dark red, double, velvety flowers measure up to 5 inches across, borne both singly and in clusters on long stems. Vigorous plants are hardy and disease-resistant, displaying dark green, leathery leaves. Blooms continuously throughout summer, although the heaviest flush of color occurs during cool weather in early summer and early autumn. The blooms almost pass for hybrid tea roses, and are good for cutting. Mostly used for training along fence rails, up trellises, and wherever a "pillar of fire" is desirable. Not so free-flowering as Blaze, but larger flowered and a darker red, with a much heavier fragrance.

NAME Dortmund

RATING ARS 9.0.

TYPE Climber

ORIGIN Hybridized by the House of Kordes, West Germany, and introduced in 1955. A cross between *R. kordesii* and an unnamed seedling.

HEIGHT Long, trailing canes that can be trained vertically or horizontally to 10 feet.

FRAGRANCE Slight.

DESCRIPTION Pointed buds open out into strawberry red, single flowers with white centers. Each flower measures up to 4 inches across and is borne in a cluster. Starts blooming early and continues throughout the entire summer. Plants are hardy and disease-resistant, and display glossy, light green leaves. Tolerates partial shade. In the landscape it is mostly used as a single specimen since it is such a strong accent it can be overpowering. Can be kept shrub-like by pruning and allowed to trail down slopes as a slope cover, but mostly used as a climber to grow up posts, trellises, and arbors.

NAME Golden Showers

RATING ARS 6.9; AARS Award, 1957 and Gold Medal Portland, 1960.

TYPE Climber

ORIGIN Hybridized by Lammerts, California, and introduced in 1956 through Germain's Roses, California. A cross between Charlotte Armstrong and Captain Thomas.

HEIGHT 8 to 12 feet; tall, rambling habit.

FRAGRANCE Moderate.

DESCRIPTION Pointed, long buds open out into glorious daffodil-yellow, double blooms, 4 inches across. Flowers behave like grandiflora roses, borne singly and in clusters on long, almost thornless stems. The glossy, dark green, leathery leaves contrast well with the flowers. Plants are vigorous, hardy, and disease-resistant, with strong canes that need little support to keep them erect. Blooms throughout the summer. Train along fences, up trellises, and as a pillar.

NAME Joseph's Coat

RATING ARS 7.5; Gold Medal Bagatelle, 1964.

TYPE Climber

ORIGIN Hybridized by Armstrong Nurseries, California, and introduced by them in 1964. A cross between Buccaneer and Circus.

HEIGHT 6 to 8 feet; erect, climbing habit.

FRAGRANCE Slight.

DESCRIPTION Yellow and red bicolored, double blooms measure 3 inches across, and are borne in tight, generous clusters. Plants are vigorous, though somewhat tender, displaying glossy, dark green leaves. Would be much more highly rated if not so susceptible to mildew. Prolific bloomer throughout summer. A versatile rose that can be used as a shrub, pillar, or climber. Though many of the blooms are true bicolors, with red and yellow petals appearing on the same flower, some flowers may be all yellow and others all red, even on the same cluster, giving it its name, Joseph's Coat.

NAME New Dawn

RATING ARS 8.0.

TYPE Climber

ORIGIN A sport of Dr. W. Van Fleet introduced by Dreer Nursery, New York, in 1930.

HEIGHT 12 to 20 feet; tall, upright habit.

FRAGRANCE Slight.

DESCRIPTION Pink, double blooms, 3 inches across, are borne in great profusion, in small clusters on long stems. They are enhanced by glossy, dark green leaves. Continuous flowering, hardy, and disease-resistant. Popular for training over arbors, especially mixed with red, yellow, orange, and white climbers, to create a kaleidoscope of color. Suitable for cutting to make attractive, informal arrangements.

NAME Piñata

RATING ARS 7.0

TYPE Climber

ORIGIN Hybridized by S. Suzuki, Japan, and introduced in 1978 by Jackson & Perkins, Oregon. A cross between seedlings of unknown parents.

HEIGHT Up to 8 feet; semi-climbing habit.

FRAGRANCE Slight.

DESCRIPTION Oval-shaped buds of light yellow and red open into high-centered blooms of yellow edged in orange, measuring up to 3 inches across. Unusual color for a climber. Easy-to-train plants have semi-glossy, green leaves. Heavy flowering in cool weather. A good rose to train along low fences or up a short trellis.

NAME Red Fountain

RATING ARS 7.0.

TYPE Climber

ORIGIN Hybridized by J. B. Williams, Maryland, and introduced by Conard Pyle in 1975. A cross between Don Juan and Blaze.

HEIGHT 10 to 12 feet; upright, climbing habit.

FRAGRANCE Heavy.

DESCRIPTION Inheriting the best traits of two of the world's best climbing roses in its parentage, including the strong fragrance of Don Juan and the prolific blooming qualities of Blaze, Red Fountain is aptly named since its flowers form an almost solid pillar of cascading blooms right down to the ground. Flowers are dark red, velvety, and double; they grow up to 3 inches wide, and are grouped in clusters. Plants are vigorous and disease-resistant.

MINIATURE ROSES

Miniature roses are generally scaled-down versions of hybrid teas and floribundas, producing their diminutive flowers on dwarf plants that rarely exceed 2 feet in height. Under ideal conditions—filtered sunlight, fertile soil, and irrigation during dry spells—miniatures can be kept in flower twelve months of the year. They are most often used for edging beds and borders, also for growing in containers. Many are suitable for growing indoors as flowering house plants. Miniatures are not judged by All-America Selections, but they are rated by the American Rose Society.

Below is the miniature rose, Woman's Day.

NAME Beauty Secret

RATING ARS 9.3; Award of Excellence 1975, American Rose Society.

TYPE Miniature

ORIGIN Hybridized by Sequoia Nurseries, California, and introduced in 1964. A cross between Little Darling and Magic Wand.

HEIGHT 8 to 12 inches; moderately compact, dwarf, bushy habit.

FRAGRANCE Strong, sweet.

DESCRIPTION Pointed, cardinal red buds open to semi-double, medium red blooms. They are perfect miniatures of the Grandes Dames of roses, the hybrid teas. Glossy, leathery leaves. Prolific bloomer. Hardy. Good in semi-shade. Top cut- and exhibition flower. One of the top-rated miniatures, excellent for growing in pots and hanging baskets and as a low edging in beds and borders.

NAME Gold Coin

RATING ARS 7.5.

TYPE Miniature

ORIGIN Hybridized by Sequoia Nurseries, California, and introduced in 1967. A miniature cross between Golden Glow and Magic Wand.

HEIGHT Up to 12 inches; low-growing, dwarf, compact habit.

FRAGRANCE Moderate.

DESCRIPTION Double, 1½-inch buttercup yellow blooms resemble hybrid tea roses, but miniature. Dark, leathery leaves. Profuse bloomer. Colorfast. Vigorous grower. Good to use as an edging for low beds and borders. Also ideal for growing in pots.

NAME Green Ice

RATING ARS 7.9.

TYPE Miniature

ORIGIN Hybridized by Sequoia Nurseries, California, and introduced in 1971. A miniature cross between *Rosa wichuraiana* (the Memorial Rose) and Floradora x Jet Trail.

HEIGHT 6 to 12 inches; short, spreading, habit.

FRAGRANCE None.

DESCRIPTION Ivory white flowers in the sun turn shades of green and chartreuse in the shade. The double blossoms are 1½ inches wide and are borne in clusters. Leathery, glossy green leaves. Prolific bloomer. Disease-resistant. Easy to grow. Makes a good hanging basket and pot plant. Good cut flower and exhibition rose.

NAME Holy Toledo

RATING ARS 8.5; Award of Excellence, 1980, American Rose Society.

TYPE Miniature

ORIGIN Hybridized by Armstrong Nurseries, California, and introduced by them in 1978. A cross between Gingersnap and Magic Carrousel.

HEIGHT Up to 20 inches; bushy, dwarf habit.

FRAGRANCE Slight.

DESCRIPTION Beautiful, shapely, miniature blooms of deep apricot with a yellow-orange center. Prolific, double, 2-inch flowers. Blooms last throughout the summer. Glossy dark leaves. Vigorous grower. Sharp thorns. Excellent pot plant. Suitable for low bedding. A good plant for grafting to create a tree-form rose.

NAME Honest Abe

RATING ARS 7.3.

TYPE Miniature

ORIGIN Hybridized by Armstrong Nurseries, California, and introduced in 1978. A cross between Fairy Moss and Rubinette.

HEIGHT 10 to 12 inches; bushy, dwarf, compact habit.

FRAGRANCE Slight tea fragrance.

DESCRIPTION Mossy buds open to deep, velvety, crimson-red, double flowers, 1½ inches across, borne on short stems. Leaves are glossy. Vigorous grower. A popular miniature for growing in pots and mass bedding.

NAME Honey Moss

RATING ARS 6.2.

TYPE Miniature

ORIGIN Hybridized by Mrs. Julia A. Sudol, California, and introduced in 1977 by Armstrong Nurseries, California.

HEIGHT 10 to 12 inches; dwarf, spreading habit.

FRAGRANCE Very fragrant.

DESCRIPTION Mossy buds open to small, 1-inch double, honey-white flowers with flat petals. Leaves are dark and leathery. Mostly used as a pot plant for growing indoors. One of the best white-flowering miniatures.

NAME Luvvie

RATING ARS 6.9.

TYPE Miniature

ORIGIN Hybridized by Dee Bennett for Tiny Petals Nursery, California, and introduced in 1980. A cross between Little Darling and Over the Rainbow.

HEIGHT 10 to 12 inches; dwarf, moderately compact habit.

FRAGRANCE Only slight.

DESCRIPTION Deep coral-pink, long-lasting, double blooms measure 5/8 to 1 inch across. Dark green leaves. Good cut flower. Admired by flower arrangers for its perfectly formed mature buds that are exact miniatures of hybrid tea roses. Makes an excellent container plant.

NAME Puppy Love

RATING ARS 8.0; Award of Excellence 1979, American Rose Society.

TYPE Miniature

ORIGIN Hybridized by E. W. Schwartz, Maryland, and introduced in 1978 by Nor'East Miniature Roses, Maryland. A cross between Zorina and an unnamed seedling.

HEIGHT Up to 16 inches; dwarf, compact habit.

FRAGRANCE Slight.

DESCRIPTION Double blossoms 1 1/2 to 1 3/4 inches across are borne singly on long stems. Flower color ranges from orange to pink to coral. Leaves are glossy; plants are free-blooming. Good cut- or exhibition flower. Excellent container plant.

NAME Starina

RATING ARS 9.4; has the highest rating of any miniature rose. Also a winner of more American and international awards than any other miniature, including a 1968 Gold Medal from Japan.

TYPE Miniature

ORIGIN Hybridized by the House of Meilland, France, and introduced in 1965 by Conard Pyle Co., Pennsylvania.

HEIGHT 15 to 18 inches; compact, dwarf, bushy habit. Climbing Starina, a mutation of Starina, grows to 4 feet.

FRAGRANCE None.

DESCRIPTION In the bud stage Starina looks like a perfect miniature of a hybrid tea rose, but opens out into cheerful, flat, double, orange-scarlet flowers that measure up to 2 inches across, borne singly and in clusters. The glossy, dark green leaves are a perfect contrast to the flowers that seem to glow like hot coals. Outstanding from bud formation to petal drop. Faded blooms just seem to stimulate more buds to develop and open for a non-stop flower show even through hot summers. Beautiful cut flower to make dainty arrangements. One of the best roses to consider for edging beds and borders as a low hedge. Makes a stunning pot plant—including hanging baskets.

HEDGE ROSES

This group is not officially recognized by the American Rose Society, since many types of roses can be planted to make a hedge effect, including miniatures and floribundas. In some catalogs and books, hedge roses are listed under shrub roses or polyantha roses. The varieties listed here are particularly good for creating flowering hedges because of the sheer quantity of their blooms. However, readers should look under other classifications for good hedging material, particularly among the species roses where the rugosa and multiflora roses are described.

NAME The Fairy

RATING ARS 8.7.

TYPE Polyanthus rose

ORIGIN Hybridized by Ann and J. A. Bentall and introduced in 1932 by Conard Pyle Co., Pennsylvania. A cross between Paul Crampel and Lady Gay.

HEIGHT 3 feet; bushy, spreading, cascading habit.

FRAGRANCE Moderate.

DESCRIPTION The pale pink flowers are small—just 1 inch across—but are produced in big clusters throughout the summer, with incredible flushes of bloom during the cool weather of early summer and early autumn. A vigorous plant, The Fairy has shiny, bright green leaves. Sometimes planted singly as a flowering shrub in mixed borders, but more often used as a low hedge or trained along fence rails. Also can be used as a slope cover for erosion control.

NAME Robin Hood

RATING ARS 7.1.

TYPE Shrub rose

ORIGIN Hybridized by the House of Pemberton, England, in 1927. A cross between Miss Edith Cavell and an unnamed seedling.

HEIGHT Up to 4 feet; dense, billowing, shrub-like habit.

FRAGRANCE None.

DESCRIPTION Carmine-red flowers about 1-inch across are grouped in large clusters that completely cover the plants in early summer. Extremely free-flowering, though its peak floral display is concentrated to several weeks in late spring and early summer. Arching canes create a dense, impenetrable barrier. Mostly used as a spectacular flowering hedge. Plants are hardy and disease-resistant, displaying small, medium green leaves.

NAME Sea Foam

RATING ARS 7.6; Gold Medal Rome, 1963 and other international awards.

TYPE Shrub rose

ORIGIN Hybridized by E. W. Schwartz and introduced in 1964 by Conard Pyle Co., Pennsylvania. Crosses among White Dawn and Pinocchio x White Dawn, and Pinocchio x White Dawn and Pinnocchio.

HEIGHT 3 to 4 feet; billowing, prostrate habit.

FRAGRANCE Slight.

DESCRIPTION Double white to cream flowers measure up to 2 inches across in dense clusters and arching canes. Leaves are small, shiny, dark green, and leathery. Mostly used as a low hedge, but can also be planted close to terraces and retaining walls where its flower laden canes will cascade onto steps and pathways. Can be planted on slopes for erosion control.

OLD-FASHIONED ROSES

Includes varieties of polyantha roses dating back hundreds of years that became immensely popular about 100 years ago. This popularity waned with the advent of modern hybrid roses, particularly the hybrid teas, floribundas, and grandifloras. Old-fashioned roses as a group also include roses of history, such as the Gallicas, Damask Roses, and Apothecary Roses whose ancestry is lost in antiquity. These roses generally are planted today as a curiosity and for nostaglic reasons. They are much less free-flowering than modern hybrids and too ungainly for most gardens. However, they do have their place in collections of roses and in restored historical gardens.

Below is the old-fashioned rose, Apothecary Rose.

NAME Baronne Prevost

RATING ARS 7.0.

TYPE Hybrid perpetual rose

ORIGIN Introduced in 1842. Descended from other hybrid perpetuals that include Damask, China, and Bourbon Roses.

HEIGHT 4 to 5 feet; bushy, erect habit.

FRAGRANCE Moderate.

DESCRIPTION Hybrid perpetuals are the forerunners of modern roses. They peaked in popularity at the end of the nineteenth century after more than 3,000 varieties were developed. Baronne Prevost is known for its profuse blooming, the main flush of color occurring in early summer, followed by a mild flush in autumn at the return of cool weather. The rose-pink, double flowers usually have an enormous number of petals, and are borne in clusters on erect stems. Plants are vigorous and hardy, with medium green foliage. Mostly used as a specimen shrub in old gardens where a carefree, informal appearance is desired.

NAME Cardinal de Richelieu

RATING ARS 7.1.

TYPE Old-fashioned

ORIGIN Developed from *Rosa gallica* in France by the House of Laffay and introduced in 1840. However, there is some evidence that it may have originated in Holland by Van Sian and named Rose Van Sian.

HEIGHT Up to 4 feet; bushy habit.

FRAGRANCE Slight.

DESCRIPTION One of the most popular old-fashioned garden roses on account of its deep purple coloring. The flowers are cup-sized, double, with in-curving petals, measuring up to 2 inches across, borne in clusters. Mostly grown as a curiosity in historical gardens as a single specimen flowering shrub.

NAME La Reine Victoria

RATING ARS 7.7.

TYPE A Bourbon rose

ORIGIN Introduced in 1872. Derived from crosses between China Roses and Damask Roses.

HEIGHT 6 feet and more; erect, spreading habit.

FRAGRANCE Wonderful apple scent.

DESCRIPTION Pure perfection of what everyone thinks an old-fashioned rose should be. The cupped, double pink flowers grow in generous clusters, each flower up to 3 inches across, nodding forward on slender stems. Plants bloom heavily in early summer, and sporadically through the growing season. Needs support such as a fence or trellis. Flowers are treasured by arrangers. Plants may need protection, such as a mulch of leaves applied after the ground freezes, where winters are severe. Best grown as an espalier, with the main canes splayed out like a fan.

NAME Martha Lambert

RATING Not rated by the American Rose Society.

TYPE Polyanthus rose (forerunner of floribunda rose)

ORIGIN Hybridized by P. Lambert, England, and introduced in 1906. A cross between Thalia and Mme Laurette Messimy.

HEIGHT 3 to 4 feet; bushy habit.

FRAGRANCE None.

DESCRIPTION Coppery rose, double blooms individually measure only $1\frac{1}{2}$ inches across, but together form large clusters of up to twenty-two roses each. An old garden rose used mostly as a short hedge or a specimen in shrub borders.

Left: The climbing rose, American Pillar, forms a colorful arbor framed over metal arches.

NAME *Rosa centifolia*

COMMON NAME Chapeau de Napoleon

RATING ARS 8.7.

TYPE Old-fashioned

ORIGIN Discovered growing on the wall of a ruined Swiss convent. Its parentage is unknown, although the flowers are similar to Moss Roses. Introduced in 1827.

HEIGHT 5 feet; arching, shrubby habit.

FRAGRANCE Moderate.

DESCRIPTION Buds have a heavy, moss-like pubescence along the flower stalks. Perfectly shaped, double pink flowers measure up to 4 inches across, and generally bloom in clusters. Medium green leaves. Plants are hardy and disease-resistant. Mostly planted to climb up a short trellis, or along an old brick or stone wall, or fence. A popular specimen to plant in historic gardens and collections of old roses.

NAME *Rosa centifolia muscosa*

COMMON NAME Moss Rose

RATING Not yet rated by the American Rose Society.

TYPE Old-fashioned

ORIGIN Introduced in the late seventeenth century, its parents descend from *Rosa centifolia,* or Cabbage Rose.

HEIGHT Usually 5 feet, but can reach 10 feet; erect, shrubby habit.

FRAGRANCE Moderate.

DESCRIPTION Named for the minute, moss-like hairs that cover the flower stem below the bud. This growth is sticky and has a fragrance similar to balsam fir. Most varieties have large, globular white, pink, crimson, or purple flowers with in-curving petals. Moss Roses usually bloom once a year, in early summer. The canes turn from red to green with age and have long thorns. Taller varieties need support. Leaves are rough, large, dark blue-green. To encourage a bushy habit cut back canes by one third after plant has flowered. Mostly grown in herb gardens and historical gardens.

NAME *Rosa damascena*

COMMON NAME Damask Rose

RATING Not yet rated by the American Rose Society.

TYPE Old-fashioned European garden rose

ORIGIN Introduced into Europe in the sixteenth century from Damascus, in what is today, Syria. Probably derived from the Red Apothecary Rose.

HEIGHT Generally 4 to 5 feet, but can grow to 8 feet in rich soil; beautiful, arching habit.

FRAGRANCE Classic rose scent. Powerful is the only word to describe it. The variety Kazanlik is the main source in the world for the extracted oil known as "Attar of Roses". More than 32,000 flowers are processed to produce one ounce of attar.

DESCRIPTION The canes are thorny, with weak, pale green stems. The flowers are double, white, pink, or red, up to 4 inches across. They grow in clusters on long stems surrounded by gray-green leaves. It blooms once a year, in early summer, except for the Autumn Damask Rose which repeats its bloom in autumn. The scarlet hips are large and round. Plants are hardy and disease-resistant. To maintain a bushy habit, remove the twiggy growth and cut back the lateral canes to three buds.

SPECIES ROSES

These are wild roses that are useful to consider for special effects and for wild gardens. For example, the sheer profusion and height of bloom from *R. banksiae* (Lady Bank's Rose) and *R. laevigata* (Cherokee Rose) endears these roses to Southern gardeners who like to grow them over arbors. The glowing red thorns of *R. sericea pteracantha* (Omei Rose) bring color to bleak winter gardens and the salt tolerance of *R. rugosa* (Rugosa Rose) allows windswept coastal gardens summertime color where few other flowering plants will survive. There are more than 200 species of roses worldwide, most have single flowers possessing five petals, but their diversity is astonishing.

Below is the species rose, *Rosa banksiae* (Lady Banks Rose).

NAME *Rosa alba*

COMMON NAME White Rose of York

RATING Not presently rated by the American Rose Society.

TYPE Species rose

ORIGIN Origin unkown. Cultivated prior to 100 A.D.

HEIGHT 6 to 8 feet; bushy habit.

FRAGRANCE Moderate.

DESCRIPTION The original plant has single, white, five-petaled flowers. Other varieties are semi-double and double, up to 3 inches across, some with petals flushed pink or yellow. The hips are conspicuous and turn scarlet in autumn. Plants are hardy and disease-resistant, with blue-green foliage. Can survive well into Canada without winter protection. Historically, *Rosa alba* is associated with the White Rose of York, made famous as a heraldic symbol during England's War of the Roses.

NAME *Rosa banksiae*

COMMON NAME Lady Banks Rose

RATING ARS 9.0.

TYPE Species rose

ORIGIN Introduced in 1796, from China.

HEIGHT To 20 feet and more; climbing habit. Can be kept bushy and shrub-like by rigorous pruning.

FRAGRANCE Slightly fragrant.

DESCRIPTION One of the few roses that will tolerate shade, though it prefers full sun. Numerous clusters of white or yellow flowers appear on slender stems, each flower no more than 1 inch across. The variety Lutea is a favorite of Southern gardeners, possessing double yellow flowers. Normalis has single white flowers, Albo Plena has double white flowers. Not reliably hardy in the northeastern United States above Washington, DC. Popular for growing over a high wall and covering romantic arbors, flowering in spring. This is the highest-rated of species roses. Plants are highly disease-resistant; evergreen leaves are small and have a medium green color; stems are almost thornless.

NAME *Rosa canina*

COMMON NAME Dog Rose, Briar Rose

RATING Not yet rated by the American Rose Society.

TYPE Species rose

ORIGIN Native to Europe; introduced into the United States prior to 1737.

HEIGHT Up to 10 feet; mounded habit.

FRAGRANCE None.

DESCRIPTION Single, white or pale pink flowers measure up to 2 inches across. They bloom throughout summer on strong, arching canes. Scarlet, conspicuous rose hips cover the plants in autumn. Leaves are medium green. Has naturalized in many parts of North America. Mostly grown as a curiosity in historical gardens. Because of the extreme hardiness of its roots, it is often used as an understock for grafting hybrids.

NAME *Rosa chinensis viridiflora*

COMMON NAME The Green Rose

RATING 7.1.

TYPE Species rose

ORIGIN China, cultivated in Europe and North America prior to 1845.

HEIGHT Usually no more than 2 feet high; weak plants have a low, bushy habit.

FRAGRANCE None.

DESCRIPTION Vivid green, double flowers, with pointed petals, barely distinguishable in color from the leaves when seen from a distance. Some color variation depending on age of plants and exposure to sunlight, some flowers tinged with bronze, others tending towards lime green. Flowers are 1 1/2 inches across, borne in generous clusters. Very little ornamental value. Mostly grown in pots as a novelty or curiosity.

NAME *Rosa foetida*

COMMON NAME Austrian Briar Rose

RATING Though the copper-red colored species has not been rated by the American Rose Society, the bicolor form is rated 8.1 and the yellow form is rated 7.7.

TYPE Species rose

ORIGIN Probably from Persia originally, but has been cultivated in Europe since the thirteenth century.

HEIGHT Up to 8 feet; erect, sparse habit.

FRAGRANCE Sickly sweet, disagreeable odor.

DESCRIPTION Single, cup-shaped, coppery red or bright yellow flowers bloom along slender, arching canes. There is a bicolored form considered to be the first bicolored rose, with the mutation occuring in the thirteenth century. Prone to blackspot disease, which discolors its blue-green leaves. Mostly grown against old stone walls, barn siding, and to disguise garden boundaries where the discoloration of its leaves is not too noticeable.

NAME *Rosa glauca.* Sometimes listed as *Rosa rubrifolia.*

COMMON NAME Redleaf Rose

RATING ARS 8.8.

TYPE Species rose

ORIGIN Introduced in 1830. Native habitat is dry mountain meadows at altitudes of 1,650 to 5,000 feet in central and southern Europe.

HEIGHT 5 feet; arching, shrubby habit.

FRAGRANCE None.

DESCRIPTION Small, single, pink flowers with yellow stamens are borne singly and in clusters of two or three. Flowering occurs in early summer, followed by decorative, bright red rose hips. Reddish tinged foliage is highly decorative, and when in full flower the plant is beautiful. Plants are hardy. The branches are used in floral arrangements.

NAME *Rosa* x *harisonii*

COMMON NAME Harison's Yellow Rose

RATING ARS 7.6.

TYPE Species rose

ORIGIN Probably a natural cross between *R. foetida* (Austrian Briar Rose) and *R. spinosissima* (Scotch Rose). Introduced in 1830 from the garden of Mr. G. F. Harison, located in what is now Midtown Manhattan, New York City, New York.

HEIGHT 6 feet and more; erect, rambling habit.

FRAGRANCE Strong, yeasty aroma.

DESCRIPTION Small, open, semi-double, bright yellow blossoms up to 2 inches across, appear in early summer. Delicate, gray-green foliage. Brownish rose hips. Plants are extremely hardy and loved by gardeners who want to grow a "cottage garden", where informality and bright color is desired. Mostly planted to grow up a trellis as an espalier, also against an old brick wall, and spilling over hedges.

NAME *Rosa hugonis*

COMMON NAME Father Hugo's Rose

RATING ARS 9.1.

TYPE Species rose

ORIGIN Probably from China, introduced in 1899.

HEIGHT 6 to 8 feet with similar spread; mounded, shrub-like habit.

FRAGRANCE None.

DESCRIPTION Brilliant, light yellow, semi-double flowers $2^3/_4$ inches wide, are borne in clusters on weeping canes. Blooms once a year in early spring, the flowers almost completely hiding the gray-green leaves. Scarlet-red hips ripen in autumn. Mostly grown as a specimen shrub in a mixed shrub or mixed perennial border. Looks sensational in old gardens, especially when planted against old brick, old stone, or old barn siding. Especially beautiful when its canes are allowed to spill over retaining walls.

NAME *Rosa laevigata*

COMMON NAME Cherokee Rose

RATING ARS 7.0.

TYPE Species rose

ORIGIN Native to China, introduced into Western gardens in 1759. Famous as the state flower of Georgia.

HEIGHT 15 to 50 feet; rambling, climbing habit.

FRAGRANCE Scent of gardenias.

DESCRIPTION Single, white flowers up to 5 inches across have conspicuous golden stamens, and are closely set along arching canes. There is also a pale pink form. Flowers profusely for about two weeks in spring. Glossy, dark green foliage helps accentuate the pure white blooms. Naturalized throughout the South where it scrambles high into the branches of towering live oak trees and loblolly pines. Not hardy in cold climates. Ideal for a trellis or arbor.

NAME *Rosa moyesii*

COMMON NAME Moyes Rose

RATING Not presently rated by the American Rose Society.

TYPE Species rose

ORIGIN Originally from Western China, introduced to the Western world in 1903.

HEIGHT 10 to 13 feet, with an equal spread; bushy, mounded habit.

FRAGRANCE Slight.

DESCRIPTION Single, velvety, blood-red flowers have creamy stamens, measuring up to 2¹/₂ inches across. Blooms once in early summer, followed by decorative scarlet-red rose hips. Plants are vigorous and hardy once established. Leaves are medium-green; its stems are thorny. Makes a good boundary hedge where an impenetrable barrier is needed.

NAME *Rosa multiflora*

COMMON NAME Multiflora Rose

RATING Not presently rated by the American Rose Society.

TYPE Species rose

ORIGIN Originally from China, introduced to the Western world in 1784. Naturalized to such an extent in the Northeastern United States that it is a pest, and local ordinances sometimes forbid its planting.

HEIGHT 10 to 16 feet; aggressive, billowing habit.

FRAGRANCE Slight.

DESCRIPTION Dense clusters of single, white flowers are borne in a cone shape on arching canes. Leaves are attractive, light green. Prefers acid soil. Grows vigorously during wet weather. Though the flowering period is brief, confined to about two weeks in early summer, its flowers are so numerous that the plants can look like mounds of snow. Mostly used as a barrier plant to mark the boundary of a property. Popular for wildlife and meadow gardens because its small orange-red hips attract songbirds, such as cardinals, in winter.

NAME *Rosa pomifera*

COMMON NAME Apple Rose

RATING ARS 6.3.

TYPE Species rose

ORIGIN Originally from Europe and Asia, introduced into cultivation in 1771.

HEIGHT 6 feet; shrub-like, mounded habit.

FRAGRANCE Slight.

DESCRIPTION Small clusters of dusky, pink, single flowers, 1 to 2 inches across, are followed in autumn by large, orange-red rose hips. The skin of the hips is thick and juicy and can be peeled like an orange and eaten raw like an apple, hence its common name. Popular during Colonial times and widely planted at Thomas Jefferson's restored gardens at his home, Monticello. Useful as a specimen in herb gardens, and to train along fence rails surrounding an orchard or vegetable garden.

NAME *Rosa rugosa*

COMMON NAME Rugosa Rose

RATING ARS 7.5.

TYPE Species rose

ORIGIN Native to Japan, introduced into Western gardens in 1845.

HEIGHT 5 to 7 feet; bushy habit.

FRAGRANCE Cinnamon scent.

DESCRIPTION Carmine or white, single or semi-double flowers measure up to 3½ inches across. Large, round, orange-red rose hips appear in autumn. Plants bloom all summer, the blossoms contrasting beautifully with rich, shiny, dark green, textured leaves, even though the flowering display is never profuse. Plants are hardy, disease-resistant, and highly salt tolerant. Popular as a seashore plant, especially to mark a property boundary and to stabilize shifting sand. Naturalized in many coastal areas of the Northeastern United States. Useful as a barrier hedge and windbreak.

NAME *Rosa sericea pteracantha.* (Also known as *Rosa omeiensis.)*

COMMON NAME Omei Rose.

RATING Not yet rated by the American Rose Society since it is grown mostly for its colorful stems, rather than its flowers.

TYPE Species rose

ORIGIN From Western China, introduced into cultivation in 1901.

HEIGHT Up to 6 feet; erect habit.

FRAGRANCE None.

DESCRIPTION Single white flowers are not considered sufficiently ornamental to be grown for its flowers alone. What attracts this unusual species to some garden connoisseurs is the beauty of its stems—particularly its conspicuous red thorns, which resemble wings and are translucent when backlighted by the sun. The thorns literally glow with a rich red color. Mostly grown as a single specimen where a winter color highlight is wanted.

Left: The rose garden at Swarthmore College, near Philadelphia, Pennsylvania, features a large collection of roses, including climbers and tree forms. *Right:* Roses planted in concrete containers are a prominent feature of the rose garden at Cheekwood Botanical Gardens, Nashville, Tennessee.

CHAPTER FOUR

GARDEN PLANS

CUTTING GARDEN FOR ROSES

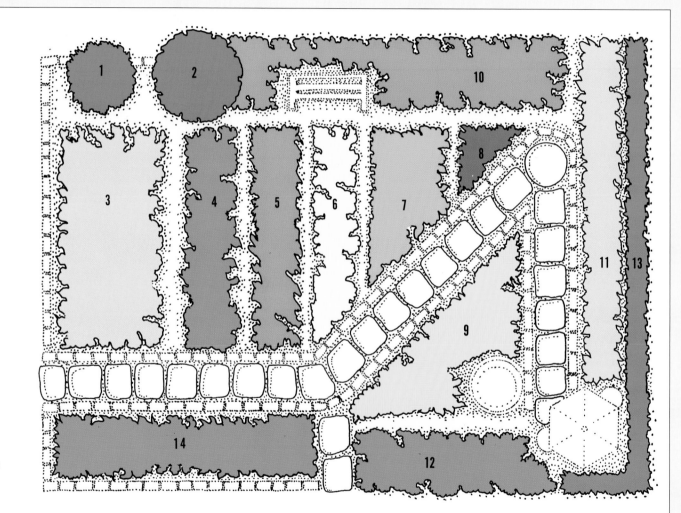

1- Grandiflora, Love
2- Climbing Rose, Blaze
3- Floribunda, Carefree Beauty
4- Floribunda, Impatient
5- Floribunda, French Lace
6- Floribunda, Marina
7- Grandiflora, Queen Elizabeth
8- Hybrid Tea, Peace
9- Hybrid Tea, Fragrant Cloud
10- Floribunda, Simplicity
11- Hybrid Tea, Dolly Parton
12- Climbing America   on trellis
13- Hybrid Tea, Tropicana
14- Hybrid Tea, Tropicana

Left: A corner of the author's rose garden, featuring the hedge rose Robin Hood and climbing Blaze.

FRAGRANCE ROSE GARDEN

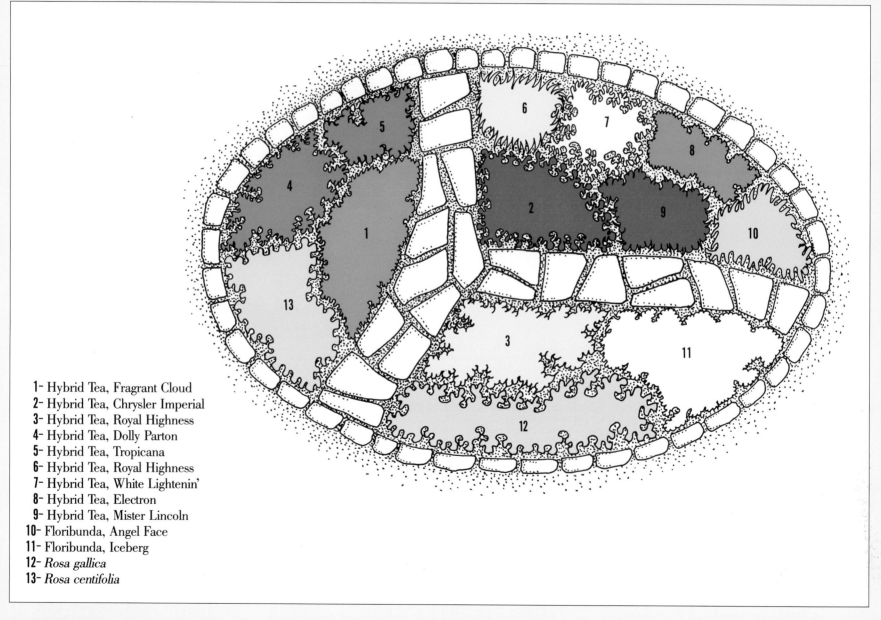

1- Hybrid Tea, Fragrant Cloud
2- Hybrid Tea, Chrysler Imperial
3- Hybrid Tea, Royal Highness
4- Hybrid Tea, Dolly Parton
5- Hybrid Tea, Tropicana
6- Hybrid Tea, Royal Highness
7- Hybrid Tea, White Lightenin'
8- Hybrid Tea, Electron
9- Hybrid Tea, Mister Lincoln
10- Floribunda, Angel Face
11- Floribunda, Iceberg
12- *Rosa gallica*
13- *Rosa centifolia*

Left: A rustic arbor and a white picket fence add an old-fashioned aura to this formal rose garden composed mostly of floribunda roses and climbing roses.

FLORIBUNDA ROSES

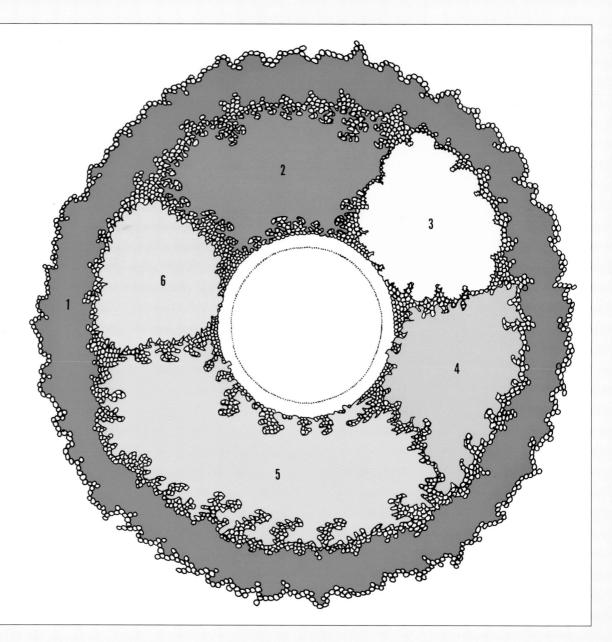

1- Miniature Starina for edging
2- Impatient
3- French Lace
4- Tropicana
5- Sun Flare
6- Gene Boerner

Left: Otto Linne, classified as a shrub rose, creates a wonderful hedge in the International Rose Test Garden, Portland, Oregon.

FORMAL PARTERRE GARDEN OF FLORIBUNDA ROSES

1- Accent
2- Charisma
3- First Edition
4- Simplicity
5- French Lace
6- Gene Boerner
7- Betty Prior
8- Impatient
9- Marina
10- Fashion
11- Iceberg
12- Showbiz
13- Fire King
14- Ivory Fashion
15- Showbiz
16- Sunsprite
17- Vogue

Left: An overview of the International Rose Test Garden in Portland, Oregon, where roses bloom continuously from mid-June until fall frost.

OLD-FASHIONED ROSE GARDEN

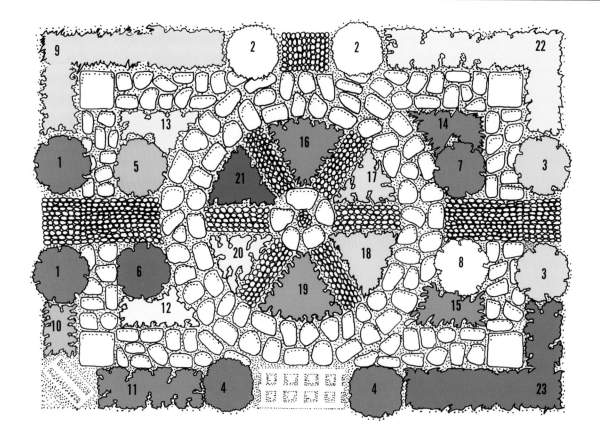

1- Climbing Rose, Blaze
2- Climbing Rose, City of York
3- Climbing Rose, Golden Showers
4- Climbing Rose, America
5- Grandiflora, Shreveport
6- Grandiflora, Queen Elizabeth
7- Grandiflora, Love
8- Grandiflora, White Lightnin'

9- Floribunda, Simplicity
10- Floribunda, Marina
11- Floribunda, Showbiz
12- Floribunda, French Lace
13- Floribunda, Gene Boerner
14- Floribunda, Betty Prior
15- Floribunda, Impatient
16- Hybrid Tea, Double Delight

17- Hybrid Tea, Chicago Peace
18- Hybrid Tea, King's Ransom
19- Hybrid Tea, Fragrant Cloud
20- Hybrid Tea, Color Magic
21- Hybrid Tea, Christian Dior
22- Hybrid Tea, The Fairy
23- Hybrid Tea, Robin Hood

Left: A corner of the old-fashioned rose garden in the herb garden at the US National Arboretum, Washington, DC. This section is planted exclusively with old-fashioned roses.

Right: The climbing rose, Blaze, is a favorite for covering garden structures, such as this archway, leading into a home garden.

CHAPTER FIVE

PLANT SELECTION GUIDES

THE FOLLOWING LIST SHOULD BE HELPFUL IN deciding which roses to choose for a particular purpose. Not only have the top 100 roses in the encyclopedia section been classified according to color, they have been listed according to suitability as bedding plants or container culture, for growing up arbors and trellises, for grounding cover effect, hedging, fragrance, repeat bloom, and many other useful purposes.

RED ROSES

HYBRID TEA
Christian Dior
Chrysler Imperial
Command Performance
Fragrant Cloud
Mister Lincoln
Olympiad
Red Masterpiece

FLORIBUNDA
Accent
Fire King
Impatient
Meidiland Scarlet
Showbiz

GRANDIFLORA
Scarlet Knight

SPECIES ROSES
Rosa foetida (Austrian Briar Rose)
Rosa moyesii (Moyes Rose)
Rosa rugosa (Rugosa Rose)

CLIMBING ROSES
Blaze (also called Improved Paul's Scarlet)
Don Juan
Dortmund
Red Fountain

MINIATURE ROSES
Beauty Secret
Honest Abe
Starina

HEDGE ROSES
Robin Hood

OLD-FASHIONED
Damask Rose
Moss Rose
Rosa gallica (Apothecary Rose)

YELLOW & ORANGE ROSES

HYBRID TEA
Brandy
King's Ransom
Medallion
Oregold
Tropicana

FLORIBUNDA
Cathedral
First Edition
French Lace
Sunsprite

SPECIES ROSES
Rosa banksiae (Lady Banks Rose)
Rosa x *harisonii* (Harison's Yellow Rose)
Rosa hugonis (Father Hugo's Rose)

CLIMBING ROSES
Golden Showers

MINIATURE ROSES
Gold Coin
Holy Toledo

GRANDIFLORA
Arizona
Sundowner

BICOLOR ROSES

HYBRID TEA
Candy Stripe
Confidence
Double Delight
Peace
Pristine
Sutter's Gold

FLORIBUNDA
Charisma

SPECIES ROSES
Rosa foetida (Austrian
  Briar Rose)

GRANDIFLORA
Love
Shreveport

CLIMBING ROSES
American Pillar
Joseph's Coat
Piñata

MINIATURE ROSES
Magic Carousel
Puppy Love

PINK ROSES

HYBRID TEA
Candy Stripe
Color Magic
Chicago Peace
Electron
Miss All-American Beauty
Perfume Delight
Pink Peace
Royal Highness

FLORIBUNDA
Betty Prior
Fashion
Gene Boerner
Meidiland Bonica
Meidiland Ferdy
Simplicity
Vogue

GRANDIFLORA
Queen Elizabeth

SPECIES ROSES
Rosa canina (Dog Rose, Briar Rose)
Rosa laevigata (Cherokee Rose)
Rosa pomifera (Apple Rose)
Rosa rubrifolia (Redleaf Rose)

CLIMBING ROSES
Constance Spry
New Dawn
Climbing Tropicana

MINIATURE ROSES
Luvvie

HEDGE ROSES
The Fairy

OLD-FASHIONED
Baronne Prevost
Chapeau de Napoleon
Damask Rose
Moss Rose

BLUE & LAVENDER ROSES

HYBRID TEA
Blue Moon

OLD-FASHIONED
Cardinal de Richelieu
Moss Rose

WHITE ROSES

HYBRID TEA
Garden Party
Honor
Pascali
White Masterpiece

FLORIBUNDA
Iceberg
Ivory Fashion
Meidiland White

GRANDIFLORA
White Lightnin'

SPECIES ROSES
Rosa alba (White Rose of York)
Rosa canina (Dog Rose, Briar Rose)
Rosa laevigata (Cherokee Rose)
Rosa multiflora (Multiflora Rose)
Rosa omeiensis (Omei Rose)

CLIMBING ROSES
City of York

HEDGE ROSES
Sea Foam

MINIATURE ROSES
Green Ice
Honey Moss

OLD-FASHIONED
Damask Rose
Moss Rose

ROSES FOR BEDDING

HYBRID TEA
Candy Stripe
Chicago Peace
Christian Dior
Chrysler Imperial
Command Performance
Electron
Garden Party
King's Ransom
Medallion
Miss All-American Beauty
Mister Lincoln
Oregold
Pascali
Peace
Perfume Delight
Royal Highness
Sutter's Gold
Tropicana

SPECIES ROSES
Rosa x *harisonii* (Harison's Yellow Rose)
Rosa rugosa (Rugosa Rose)

FLORIBUNDA
Betty Prior
Fashion
Gene Boerner
Iceberg
Vogue

GRANDIFLORA
Arizona
Queen Elizabeth
Scarlet Knight

MINIATURE ROSES
Beauty Secret
Puppy Love
Starina

OLD-FASHIONED
Damask Rose
La Reine Victoria
Chapeau de Napoleon
Martha Lambert

ROSES FOR CONTAINERS

HYBRID TEA
Pascali

FLORIBUNDA
First Edition
French Lace

MINIATURE ROSES
Beauty Secret
Green Ice
Luvvie
Puppy Love

ROSES FOR GROUND COVER

CLIMBING ROSES
Dortmund
New Dawn

HEDGE ROSES
Sea Foam
The Fairy

MINIATURE ROSES
Beauty Secret
Gold Coin
Holy Toledo

ROSES FOR HEDGING

HYBRID TEA
Command Performance
Medallion
Pink Peace

FLORIBUNDA
Betty Prior
Charisma
First Edition
Gene Boerner
Iceberg
Ivory Fashion
Meidiland
Simplicity
Sunsprite
Vogue

GRANDIFLORA
Arizona
Queen Elizabeth

SPECIES ROSES
Rosa alba (White Rose of York)
Rosa x *harisonii* (Harison's Yellow Rose)
Rosa moyesii (Moyes Rose)
Rosa rugosa (Rugosa Rose)

HEDGE ROSES
The Fairy
Robin Hood
Sea Foam

MINIATURE ROSES
Gold Coin
Luvvie
Starina

OLD-FASHIONED
La Reine Victoria
Rosa gallica (Apothecary Rose)
Chapeau de Napoleon
Martha Lambert

Opposite page: The old-fashioned rose, La Reine Victoria, trained against a fence. First introduced in 1872, the delicate, pink-cupped flowers are highly fragrant.

Opposite page: The climbing rose, Tropicana, is trained to climb a pillar by having its long canes tied upright to the support by means of "twist-ties." The original Tropicana is a hybrid tea. Both forms have a delightful fruity fragrance.

ROSES FOR REPEAT BLOOMS

HYBRID TEA
Candy Stripe
Chicago Peace
Christian Dior
Confidence
Double Delight
Electron
Fragrant Cloud
Garden Party
Honor
King's Ransom
Medallion
Meidiland
Miss All-American Beauty
Mister Lincoln
Olympiad
Oregold
Paradise
Pascali
Peace
Perfume Delight
Pink Peace
Red Masterpiece
Simplicity
Sutter's Gold
Tropicana
White Masterpiece

FLORIBUNDA
Betty Prior
Charisma
Fashion
Fire King
First Edition
French Lace
Gene Boerner
Iceberg
Impatient
Sunsprite

GRANDIFLORA
Love
Queen Elizabeth
Scarlet Knight
Sundowner
White Lightenin'

CLIMBING
Blaze
City of York
Dortmund
Don Juan
The Fairy
Golden Showers
Joseph's Coat
New Dawn
Piñata
Red Fountain

MINIATURE
Beauty Scarlet
Green Ice
Holy Toledo
Puppy Love
Starina

HEDGE
Robin Hood

OLD-FASHIONED
Baronne Prevost
La Reine Victoria
Moss Rose

SPECIES
Rosa alba (White Rose of York)
Rosa rugosa (Rugosa Rose)

ROSES FOR ARBORS & TRELLISES

CLIMBING
American Pillar
Blaze
City of York
Don Juan
Dortmund
Fragrant Cloud
Golden Showers
Joseph's Coat
New Dawn
Piñata
Red Fountain

HEDGE
Sea Foam

OLD-FASHIONED
Damask Rose

SPECIES
Rosa foetida (Austrian Briar Rose)
Rosa laevigata (Cherokee Rose)
Rosa moyesii (Moyes Rose)

ROSES FOR FRAGRANCE

HYBRID TEA
Blue Moon
Chrysler Imperial
Command Performance
Confidence
Double Delight
Electron
Fragrant Cloud
Miss All-American Beauty
Mister Lincoln
Perfume Delight
Pink Peace
Red Masterpeice
Royal Highness
Sutter's Gold
Tropicana

FLORIBUNDA
Betty Prior
Cathedral
Fashion
Iceberg
Ivory Fashion
Sunsprite

GRANDIFLORA
Arizona
Queen Elizabeth
Sundowner
White Lightenin'

CLIMBING
City of York
The Fairy
Golden Showers
Red Fountain

MINIATURE
Beauty Secret
Magic Carousel

OLD-FASHIONED
Chapeau de Napoleon
Baronne Prevost
Damask Rose
La Reine Victoria
Moss
Rosa gallica (Apothecary Rose)

SPECIES
Rosa alba (White Rose of York)
Rosa foetida (Austrian
   Briar Rose)
Rosa x *harisonii* (Harison's
   Yellow Rose)
Rosa laevigata (Cherokee Rose)
Rosa rugosa (Rugosa Rose)

ROSES FOR SEASHORE

CLIMBING
American Pillar

SPECIES
Rosa rugosa (Rugosa Rose)

ALL-AMERICA ROSE SELECTIONS WINNERS

1940
Dicksons Red
Flash
The Chief
World's Fair

1941
Apricot Queen
California
Charlotte Armstrong

1942
Heart's Desire

1943
Grande Duchesse Charlotte
Mary Margaret McBride

1944
Fred Edmunds
Katherine T. Marshall
Lowell Thomas
Mme. Chiang Kai-shek
Mme. Marie Curie

1945
Floradora
Horace McFarland
Mirandy

1946
Peace

1947
Rubaiyat

1948
Diamond Jubilee
High Noon
Nocturne
Pinkie
San Fernando
Taffeta

1949
Forty-niner
Tallyho

1950
Capistrano
Fashion
Sutter's Gold
Mission Bells

1951
No Selection

1952
Fred Howard
Helen Traubel
Vogue

1953
Chrysler Imperial
Ma Perkins

1954
Lilibet
Mojave

1955
Jiminy Cricket
Queen Elizabeth
Tiffany

1956
Circus

1957
Golden Showers
White Bouquet

1958
Fusilier
Gold Cup
White Knight

1959
Ivory Fashion
Starfire

1960
Fire King
Garden Party
Sarabande

1961
Duet
Pink Parfait

1962
Christian Dior
Golden Slippers
John S. Armstrong
King's Ransom

1963
Royal Highness
Tropicana

1964
Granada
Saratoga

1965
Camelot
Mister Lincoln

1966
American Heritage
Apricot Nectar
Matterhorn

1967
Bewitched
Gay Princess
Lucky Lady
Roman Holiday

1968
Europeana
Miss All-American Beauty
Scarlet Knight

1969
Angel Face
Comanche
Gene Boerner
Pascali

1970
First Prize

1971
Aquarius
Command Performance
Redgold

1972
Apollo
Portrait

1973
Electron
Gypsy
Medallion

1974
Bahia
Bon Bon
Perfume Delight

1975
Arizona
Oregold
Rose Parade

1976
America
Cathedral
Seashell
Yankee Doodle

1977
Double Delight
First Edition
Prominent

1978
Charisma
Color Magic

1979
Friendship
Paradise
Sundowner

1980
Love
Honor
Cherish

1981
Bing Crosby
Marina
White Lightenin'

1982
Brandy
French Lace
Mon Cheri
Shreveport

1983
Sun Flare
Sweet Surrender

1984
Impatient
Intrigue
Olympiad

1985
Showbiz

1986
Broadway
Touch of Class
Voo Doo

1987
Bonica
New Year
Sheer Bliss

1988
Amber Queen
Mikado
Prima Donna

1989
Debut
Tournament of Roses
Class Act
New Beginning

Opposite page: Perfect shape is seen in this close-up of a specimen of Christian Dior, a hybrid tea rose.

HARDINESS ZONE CHART

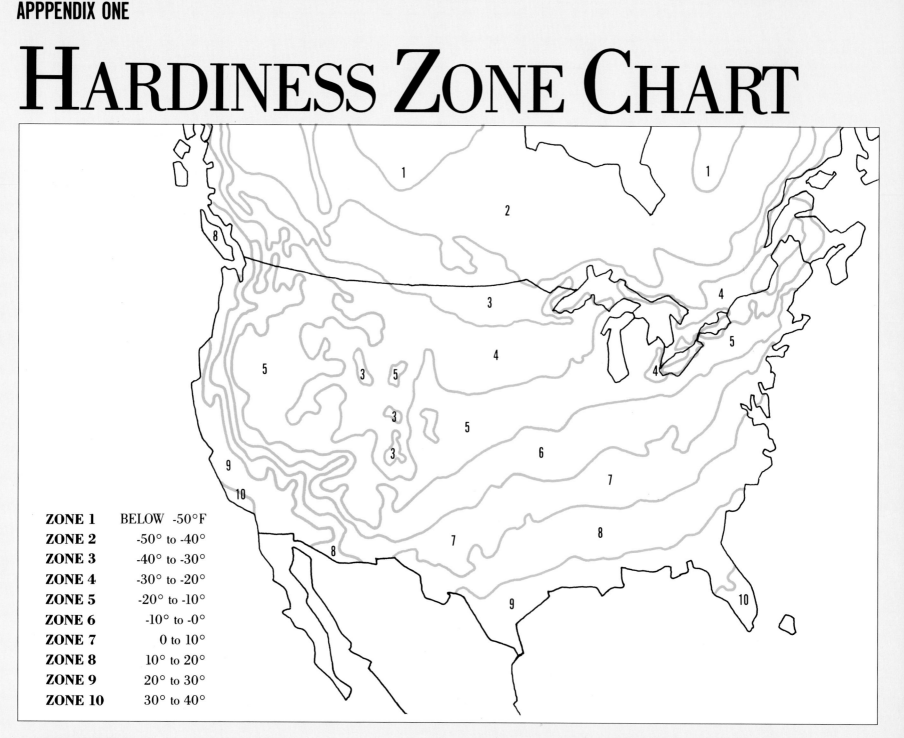

ZONE 1	BELOW -50°F
ZONE 2	-50° to -40°
ZONE 3	-40° to -30°
ZONE 4	-30° to -20°
ZONE 5	-20° to -10°
ZONE 6	-10° to -0°
ZONE 7	0 to 10°
ZONE 8	10° to 20°
ZONE 9	20° to 30°
ZONE 10	30° to 40°

Left: This city garden in the historic area of Charleston, South Carolina, is highlighted with a colonial-style arbor covered with yellow Lady Banks roses, a species rose popular in southern gardens.

SOURCES

ROSES (MODERN)

ARMSTRONG ROSES
P.O. Box 1020
Somis, CA 93066
Catalog free

BDK NURSERY
P. O. Box 628
2091 Haas Rd.
Apopka, FL 32712
Catalog free

EMLONG NURSERIES
2671 W. Marquette Woods Rd.
Stevensville, MI 49127
Catalog free

GURNEY SEED & NURSERY COMPANY
2nd & Capital
Yankton, SD 57078
Catalog free

HASTINGS
P. O. Box 4274
Atlanta, GA 30302-4274
Catalog free

HORTICO, INCORPORATED
723 Robson Rd., R.R. 1
Waterdown, ON, Canada L0R2H0
Catalog free

JACKSON & PERKINS COMPANY
P. O. Box 1028
Medford, OR 97501
Catalog free

KRIDER NURSERIES
P. O. Box 29
Middlebury, IN 46540
Catalog free

McCONNELL NURSERIES, INCORPORATED
R. R. 1
Port Burwell, ON, Canada N0J1T0
Catalog free

MILAEGER'S GARDENS
4838 Douglas Ave.
Racine, WI 53402-2498
Catalog $1.00.

ROSE ACRES
6641 Crystal Blvd.
Diamond Springs, CA 95619
Catalog free with 9½" long self-addressed envelope.

ROSES BY FRED EDMUNDS
6235 S. W. Kahle Rd.
Wilsonville, OR 97070
Catalog free

SAVAGE FARMS NURSERY
P. O. Box 125
Highway 56 South
McMinnville, TN 37110
Catalog free

SPRING HILL NURSERIES COMPANY
P. O. Box 1758
Peoria, IL 61656
Catalog free

STARK BROTHERS NURSERIES & ORCHARD COMPANY
Highway 54 West
Louisiana, MO 63353-0010
Catalog free

THOMASVILLE NURSERIES
P. O. Box 7
1842 Smith Avenue
Thomasville, GA 31799-0007
Catalog free

WAYSIDE GARDENS
P. O. Box 1
Hodges, SC 29695-0001
Catalog $1.00

ROSES (MINIATURE)

ARMSTRONG ROSES
P. O. Box 1020
Somis, CA 93066
Catalog free

JUSTICE MINIATURE ROSES
5947 S. W. Kahle Rd.
Wilsonville, OR 97070
Catalog free

MB FARM MINIATURE ROSES
Jamison Hill Rd.
Clinton Corners, NY 12514
Catalog free

McDANIEL'S MINIATURE ROSES
7523 Zemco Street
Lemon Grove, CA 92045
Catalog free

MINI-ROSES
P. O. Box 4255, Sta. A
Dallas, TX 75208
Catalog free

MINIATURE PLANT KINGDOM
4125 Harrison Grade Rd.
Sebastopol, CA 95472
Catalog $2.50

NOR' EAST MINIATURE
ROSES
58 Hammond Street
Rowley, MA 01969
Catalog free

THE ROSE GARDEN & MINI
ROSE NURSERY
P. O. Box 560
SC Highway 560 (Austin Street)
Cross Hill, SC 29332-0560
Catalog free

ROSEHILL FARM
Gregg Neck Road
Galena, MD 21635
Catalog free

TINY PETALS NURSERY
489 Minot Avenue
Chula Vista, CA 92010
Catalog free

ROSES
(OLD GARDEN & SPECIES)

ANTIQUE ROSE EMPORIUM
Route 5, Box 143
Brenham, TX 77833
Catalog $2.00

GREENMANTLE NURSERY
3010 Ettersburg Rd.
Garberville, CA 95440
Catalog $3.00

HERITAGE ROSARIUM
211 Haviland Mill Rd.
Brookville, MD 20833
Catalog $1.00

HERITAGE ROSE GARDENS
16831 Mitchell Creek Drive
Ft. Bragg, CA 95437
Catalog $1.00

HIGH COUNTRY ROSARIUM
1717 Downing Street
Denver, CO 80218
Catalog $1.00

HISTORICAL ROSES
1657 W. Jackson St.
Painesville, OH 44077
*Catalog free with 9½" long
self-addressed envelope*

LOWE'S OWN-ROOT ROSES
6 Sheffield Rd.
Nashua, NH 03062
Catalog $2.00

PICKERING NURSERIES
INCORPORATED
670 Kingston Rd. (Hwy. 2)
Pickering, ON, Canada L1V1A6
Catalog $2.00

ROSES OF YESTERDAY & TODAY
802 Brown's Valley Rd.
Watsonville, CA 95076-0398
Catalog $2.00

INDEX OF BOTANICAL AND COMMON NAMES

Page numbers in italics refer to captions and illustrations.

Accent, 53
All-America Rose Selections, 18, 20
    winners, 120-21
America, *22-23*
American Pillar, 69, 74
American Rose Society, 20
    miniature rose award of, 18
    rating system, 14
Anatomy of roses, *16*
Apothecary Rose. *See Rosa centifolia provincialis*
Apple Rose. *See Rosa pomifera*
Arbors, roses for, 118
Austrian Briar Rose. *See Rosa foetida*

Bare-root roses, 13
Baronne Prevost, 85
Beauty Secret, 77
Bedding, roses for, 117
Betty Prior, 53
Bicolor roses, list of, 114
Blackspot fungus, 26
Blaze, 69, *101, 110*
Blooming period, 21
Blue Moon, 35
Blue roses, list of, 114
Brandy, 35
Briar Rose. *See Rosa canina*

Candy Stripe, 36
Cardinal de Richelieu, 85
Cathedral, 54
Chapeau de Napoleon. *See Rosa centifolia*
Charisma, 54

Cherokee Rose. *See Rosa laevigata*
Chicago Peace, 36
Christian Dior, 37, *120*
Chrysler Imperial, 37
City of York, *24*, 70
Classifications, 15-18
Climbing roses, 68-75
    definition and description, 15
    pruning of, 29
Color lists, 113-15
Color Magic, 38
Command Performance, 38
Confidence, 39
Conard Pyle Company, 19-20
Constance Spry, *14-15*, 68, 70
Containers
    growing in, 21
    roses for, 117
Cutting garden, 100
Cypress Gardens (South Carolina), *114-15*

Damask rose. *See Rosa damascena*
Diseases, 26
Dog Rose. *See Rosa canina*
Dolly Parton, 39
Don Juan, 71
Dortmund, 71
Double Delight, 40

Electron, 40

The Fairy, 82
Fashion, 55
Father Hugo's Rose. *See Rosa hugonis*
Feeding, 21, 24
Fertilizing, 24
Fire King, 55

First Edition, 56
Floribunda garden, 104
Floribunda roses, 52-61
Formal parterre garden of floribunda roses, 106
Fragrance, 21
    roses for, 119
Fragrance garden, 102
Fragrant Cloud, 41
French Lace, 56
Fungi, 26

Garden Party, 41
Gene Boerner, 57
Gold Coin, 77
Grandiflora roses, 62-67
    definition and description, 15
Green Ice, 78
The Green Rose. *See Rosa chinensis viridiflora*
Ground cover, roses for, 117
Growing size, *15*
Growth areas, 21

Harison's Yellow Rose. *See Rosa x harisonii*
Hedge roses, 82-83
Hedging, roses for, 117
Height standards, 14
Heirloom, *34*
Holy Toledo, 78
Honest Abe, 79
Honey Moss, 79
Huntington Botanical Garden (California), *125*
Hybridization, *30-31*
Hybrid tea roses, 34-51
    definition and description, 15

Iceberg, 57
Impatient, 58
Improved Paul's Scarlet, 69
Insects, 21, 26
    International Rose Test Garden (Oregon), *105, 107, 112-13*
Irrigation, 26
Ivory Fashion, 58

Just Joey, *50*

King's Ransom, 42

Lady Banks Rose. *See Rosa banksiae*
La Reine Victoria, 86, *116-17*
Lavender roses, list of, 114
Longwood Gardens (Pennsylvania), *74*
Love, 62, 113
Luvvie, 80

Marina, 59
Martha Lambert, 86, *87*
Medallion, 43
Meidiland, 73
Meilland and Son, 18-20
Middleton Place Plantation (South Carolina), *81*
Miniature roses, 76-81
    definition and description, 18
Miss All-American Beauty, 43
Mister Lincoln, 44
Mites, 26
Moss rose. *See Rosa centifolia muscosa*
Moyes Rose. *See Rosa moyesii*
Mulch, 26-29
Multiflora Rose. *See Rosa multiflora*

New Dawn, *12-13*, 73

Old-fashioned garden, 108
Old-fashioned roses, 84-89
  definition and description, 18
Olympiad, 44
Omei Rose. *See Rosa sericea*
  pteracantha
Orange roses, list of, 114
Oregold, 45
Otto Linne, *105*

Paradise, 45
Pascali, 46
Peace Rose, 18-20, 46
Perfume Delight, 47
Piñata, 75
Pink Peace, 47
Pink roses, list of, 114
Planting, 23-24
Planting locations, 21
Polyantha roses, definition and
  description, 15
Popular varieties, 21
Potted roses, 13
Pristine, 48
Pruning, 21, 29
Puppy Love, 80
Purchasing, 13-14
Pyle, Robert, 19-20

Queen Elizabeth, *24*, 64, 65
Queen Victoria. *See* La Reine
Victoria

Rating system, 14
Red Fountain, 75
Redleaf Rose. *See Rosa glauca*
Red Masterpiece, 48
Red roses, list of, 113
Repeat blooms, roses for, 118
Robin Hood, 83, *101*
Rosa alba, 91
Rosa banksiae, *89*, 91, *114-15*,
  122-23
Rosa canina, 92
Rosa centifolia , 88
Rosa centifolia muscosa, 88
Rosa centifolia provincialis, 84
Rosa chinensis viridiflora, 92

Rosa damascena, 89
Rosa foetida, 93
Rosa glauca, 93
Rosa hugonis, 94
Rosa laevigata, 81, 90, 95
Rosa moyesii, 95
Rosa multiflora, 96
Rosa omeiensis. See Rosa sericea
  pteracantha
Rosa pomifera, 96
Rosa rubrifolia. See Rosa glauca
Rosa rugosa, 97
Rosa sericea pteracantha, 97
Rosa x harisonii, *94*
Rose types, *16-17*
Royal Highness, *49*
Rugosa Rose. See Rosa rugosa

Scarlet Knight, 64
Sea Foam, 83
Seashore, roses for, 119
Showbiz, 59
Shreveport, 66
Shrub roses, definition and
  description, 18
Simplicity, 32-33 , 60
Soil preparation, 23
Species roses, 90-97
  definition and description, 18
Spider mites, 26
Spraying, 21, 26
Starina, 81
Summer Sunshine, 13
Sundowner, 66
Sunsprite, 60
Sutter's Gold, 49

Transplanting, 21
Trellises, roses for, 118
Tropicana, 51, 118-19

US National Arboretum (Washington,
  DC), 109

Vogue, 61

Weeds, 26-29
White Lightnin', 67
White Masterpiece, 51
White Rose of York. *See Rosa alba*

White roses, list of, 115
Winter protection, 21
Woman's Day, 18

Yellow roses, list of, 114